THE
LIFE
AND
TIMES
OF
JIM
WALKER

COWBOY, TEXAS RANGER
AND SOLIDER

WELDON KING

iUniverse®

THE LIFE AND TIMES OF JIM WALKER
COWBOY, TEXAS RANGER AND SOLIDER

iUniverse books may be ordered through booksellers or by contacting:

iUniverse
1663 Liberty Drive
Bloomington, IN 47403
www.iuniverse.com
844-349-9409

ISBN: 978-1-6632-0111-9 (sc)
ISBN: 978-1-6632-0110-2 (e)

Library of Congress Control Number: 2020916968

Print information available on the last page.

iUniverse rev. date: 09/17/2020

PROLOGUE

The story begins with a teenage boy traveling with his family back to their home in Jackson, Mississippi from Arkansas. The time is just before the Civil War. The boy's thoughts are not on politics or various conflicts of the day. His mind is instead overwhelmed by his dream of going to Texas and becoming a cowboy and ranger. He had exciting visions of accumulating free grazing land to build a herd from the wild cattle and Spanish horses grazing on the open range. He is weighing this against the prospect of leaving his family and possibly never seeing them again. It is a decision that could change his life forever.

The teenager was riding his four-year-old filly named Charlie, completely oblivious to his present surroundings and lost in his daydreams. His favorite fantasy consisted of going to Texas and homesteading the free land. A man could homestead acreage and gather up all the free livestock, including longhorn cattle and Mexican ponies roaming free on the open range. This is what he wanted to do.

The young man's name was James Jefferson Walker, better known by those who knew him as Jim. He was big for his age, approximately six feet in height with hazel eyes full of wonderment and black hair that was closely cropped. He rode his horse Charlie along what was called a road; however, it was just a wide trail leading back from Arkansas to his hometown of Jackson, Mississippi. He was with his family which included his uncle and his cousin, Billy Roy. His cousin, next to Charlie, was his best friend and had been since early childhood.

The family had been living in Arkansas for the past two years since his father was in the lumber business and had moved to the area for business purposes. They were going home to Mississippi much to the dismay of Jim. He wanted to live out his Texas dreams.

The wagon train consisted of three wagons loaded with the furniture and personal belongings of the two families. Typically, it was the responsibility of Jim and his cousin to scout ahead to select the roads, river crossings, and act as trailblazers. This enabled the two boys to have a lot of time alone. They discussed many things with going to Texas at the top of their list. The boys, barely sixteen years old, were excited just talking about it.

They had heard about Stephen Austin and the first colonies, the Texas revolution with Sam Houston, Texas' time as an independent nation and its entry into the United States in 1846. It was not uncommon to go to a neighbor's home and see it boarded up with a sign on the front door that said GTT or "Gone to Texas." Jim repeatedly tried to convince his father they should go to the Texas frontier and grab as much of the free land as possible. Vast herds of cattle and horses from the Spanish occupation were roaming the open prairies and were there for the taking.

The excitement was difficult to contain and made the drudgery of the trail more bearable. As they reached Northeast Louisiana, the boys decided they would make one last attempt to persuade their fathers, but if this attempt was not successful, they would saddle their horses and ride of in the middle of the night for the "Promised Land."

Later, Jim asked his father if he could talk to him about some very important issues. When he brought up the subject again, his father told him he was not going to Texas and that was the end of the subject. Jim told his father he would stay with him, working the new land until it was productive or as long as he was needed. His father again refused and said he did not want to hear any more about it.

Jim called on Billy and told him what his father had said. Billy stated that his father was just as adamant about not going. Jim said he was going if he had to go alone. They came up with a plan to saddle their horses and ride off while everyone was asleep the following night. The next day they filled their saddle bags with food and what they imagined they would need to get to Texas. Each boy had a shotgun and camp and ball pistol which was also crowded into their blankets and saddle bags.

Sometime around midnight, the boys crept over to their horses while asking each other just before mounting if this was really what they wanted to do. They agreed and silently rode their horses away from the camp. A barking dog woke the family and their fathers quickly discovered their absence. They saddled their horses and took off in hot pursuit. The fathers overtook the boys as they came upon a plank fence. Jim and Billy rode their horses back so they could get a running start and jump the fence. Billy's horse could not jump the barrier, but Jim' horse, Charlie, cleared the top rail. As Jim landed on the opposite side, his father approached him. He attempted to jump the fence as well but was unable to do so. They sat on their horses and looked at each other across the fence without saying a word. Tears came to their eyes as the possibility of never seeing each other again was a real possibility. After what seemed like forever, Jim turned his horse west and rode off toward the promised land of Texas. As he rode away, the realization came over him that he may never see his family again.

1

THE JOURNEY TO TEXAS

Of course, he did not know if he would see his family again, but he was so excited to finally begin his adventure of going to Texas. He knew enough of geography to know he only had one major waterway to navigate, the Sabine River, which separated the state of Louisiana from the state of Texas.

When he left his father's wagon train, he took only those things that were his property except for some black powder and balls for his weapons. His horse Charlie was raised from a colt and was not only his private property but also his best friend. He talked to Charlie as if she was a human and Jim thought sometimes she really could understand simple conversation. She did understand commands and followed them without hesitation. Spurs were not necessary and would be considered immoral to use on Charlie. The slightest touch of the reigns against the side of her neck would result with a turn in the desired direction. He could mount from either side or a running mount from the rear with Jim putting both hands on the horse's rump and vaulting onto her back.

The love and closeness between the two became even greater as they crossed the new territory of Louisiana. The route across the state is the approximate area of what is known today as Shreveport. This was somewhat scary as Jim was alone and in a strange new world which he knew little or nothing about. It was a price he was willing to pay, however, to achieve his dream.

The year was 1860 with the war drums being beat in both the Northern and Southern tiers of the country. He had just turned sixteen, though, and had more pressing and exciting concerns to think about. He had encountered a wagon train just west of Shreveport with the wagon master informing him of a ferry spanning the Sabine River. He invited Jim to follow them and they would direct him to the crossing. This not only provided direction, but also safety. The Indians were almost non-existent in these territories; however, there were still many outlaws and highwaymen who preyed on lonely travelers.

Jim enjoyed the many friendships he made while on the train, but he had also gained much useful information about Texas from the Wagon Master, who had made many trips to the state of Texas. After crossing the river into his new country, he veered southwest down through the pine forest of East Texas toward Fort Parker. He marveled at the beautiful country, the magnificent pine forests and the rolling prairies with lush grass waist high.

The longhorn cattle and wild horses were everywhere, just waiting to be claimed and branded. Jim did not have the wherewithal to start a ranch, including the land or the money for supplies so he needed a job for a grub stake. The wagon master told him of a ranch just outside of Mexia that might be hiring. Mexia was a small town approximately two hundred miles southwest of where he entered Texas on the ferry. He decided that he would give the ranch a try but first wanted to see the fort where Cynthia Ann Parker was captured when the fort was stormed by Comanche Indians and several of her relatives were killed.

After her capture, Cynthia Ann lived with his tribe, married Chief Nocona and bore him two sons. One of these sons became the all-powerful Chief of the Comanche, Quanah Parker. Quanah terrorized Texas until he was defeated in the Battle of Palo Duro in the Texas Panhandle. He was the last powerful Indian force in Texas. After viewing the fort, Jim rode over to Mexia to seek employment. He stopped at the general store and asked about many ranchers in the area who might be hiring cow punchers. He was told the Spillar Ranch just outside of town was owned by a recent immigrant from Illinois who had started a spread and was hiring cowboys.

2

BECOMING A COWBOY

Jim thanked the storekeeper and, using the directions in a strange territory, eventually made his way to the Spillar Ranch. Reluctantly, he walked up the pathway to the main house and knocked on the front door. He had never applied for employment before and wasn't sure how to do it. But he needed money. So when Mrs. Spillar came to the door and introduced herself, he was quite impressed by her mannerism and physical beauty. She was considered to be an older lady at the time, probably at least 35 years of age. Her hair was blond and flowed off her shoulders down her back almost to her waist. She had a turned-up nose with radiant blue eyes. She was a beautiful lady.

Jim mumbled that he was looking for work as a ranch hand. She said she did not do the hiring, but her husband, who was rounding up strays, would be in toward sundown. She asked if he was hungry and he answered with a hesitating nod of his head. She provided a wash basin for him to clean up and fed him a hearty meal of stew and cornbread. This was the first good meal he'd eaten since leaving their home

4

in Arkansas. Mrs. Spillar directed him to the woodpile at the rear of the main house and showed him a chopping axe, explaining they never had enough kindling. He spent the rest of the afternoon chopping and splitting kindling wood.

Late in the afternoon, about dark, Mr. Spillar arrived back at the ranch with a few of his hands. By this time, Jim had a sizeable stack of wood chopped ready for the cook stove, fireplace, and the stove in the bunkhouse. He heard someone calling his name, and he looked up at a large man, over six feet in height with ruggedly handsome features and a kindly expression on his face.

"I'm Mr. Spillar." the man said. "I understand you're looking for a job on the ranch."

"Yes sir," Jim replied sheepishly.

"How old are you, son?" Mr. Spillar asked. "Where are you from?"

"I'm eighteen," Jim replied, stretching the truth a little, figuring that he would not get hired otherwise. "I came from Mississippi."

"You think you have the age and maturity to handle the job?" Mr. Spillar asked with a twinkle in his eye. "It's a man-sized job, son."

"I think so, sir," Jim answered.

"Well then, Jim, put your belongings in the bunkhouse and find yourself a bed," Mr. Spillar said. "I'll give you an opportunity for a few days to see if you can hack it."

Jim never looked back and, within a few months, he was a top hand. He had a string of mounts furnished by Mr. Spillar. Charlie, however, was still his number one horse and friend and that would remain so long as Charlie was alive.

The most difficult part of the cowboy job was roping off a horse. Although he had been riding horseback all his life, he had not been in a ranch environment, doing things such as riding fence, doing round-ups, or branding a roping cattle to doctor them. The foreman, Tom Green, took Jim under his wing and taught him what he needed to know in a gradual way. Before long, he was one of the best cowhands on the ranch.

3

RAIDS AND BECOMING A RANGER

One afternoon, Mr. Spillar called a meeting of all the cowhands in the big meeting room of the main house. Mr. Spillar mentioned the strong possibility of a raid conducted by a band of Mexican bandits. They had a hacienda they used as their headquarters and way station near Victoria when driving their stolen cattle and horses to Mexico. According to an informant riding with the bandits, they should arrive at the ranch at roughly midnight that very night. He asked for anyone who did not feel right about defending the ranch to stand up. No one stood up. He also asked about the viability of their firearms. Most were armed with cap and ball revolvers with a few also sporting break open shotguns.

The plans laid out by Mr. Spillar were to guard the herds by lying back in the scrub oak trees so as not to be seen until the bandits were committed. Because of Jim' age and inexperience, he was to be kept close to Tom Green, the ranch foreman. Jim was nervous and a little bit scared as he had never experienced anything of this sort. He guessed this was a small taste of what it would be like to be a Texas ranger. On this night, he would be tested to determine if he had what it takes. Yes, he was a little bit more than nervous.

Before they went out to guard the livestock, a steak supper with mashed potatoes and cream gravy was furnished to all the ranch hands by Mrs. Spillar in the big room. This was probably even better than the Sunday dinners with Momma Walker's fried chicken. Mrs. Spillar said the blessing and asked the Lord to look after and protect her husband and boys.

After dinner, the cowboys rode out to the big pasture where the cattle were grazing. There were no fences except pole fences used for corrals primarily around the barns. These corrals were utilized for catching riding horses by running the horse herd into the pen and roping a mount for the day. With no fences, the horse and cattle herds could range far from the ranch headquarters. To maintain some degree of control, the herds would be fed in certain areas. They would not stray far from these areas where they were fed and, of course, they had the Spillar brand.

Mr. Spillar and Tom Green, the ranch foreman and sometimes Texas Ranger who was experienced at disrupting bandits' lives, oversaw the surprise party. The cattle and horses were grazing in a large meadow of lush grass with feed troughs. The pasture had scrub oak trees about halfway up the side of the slight hills surrounding the meadow. Tom Green told Jim to go with him. Tom took roughly half the cowhands and went to the other side of the meadow with Mr. Spillar taking the other half to the opposite side of the large pasture.

Now it was time to simply wait. Waiting was hard for Jim as he didn't know how he would perform. Tom rode up to him and, seemingly sensing his anxieties, stated he would do fine. Tom told him to just stay close to him and not try to do too much.

Jim thought of home and what he would be doing if his horse had not been able to jump the high fence on that distant night. He checked his guns, too, more from nervousness than anything else. The moon was what they called a Comanche Moon or a full moon with relatively good nighttime visibility. However, the trees cast a shadow which could be deceiving causing an inexperienced Ranger to see things that weren't there. Despite this, Jim saw movement along the edge of the trees he was certain was bandits. He nudged Tom and pointed at the moving shadows but quickly saw it for what it was, a buck deer and his doe.

It was a chilly November night and uncomfortable just sitting in the saddle. Along about midnight, a large group of riders came in from the southwest and split up into two groups with one headed cautiously toward the herd of cattle and the other moving towards the grazing horses. The strategy, as explained to Jim while sitting on his horse and freezing, was to let the bandits trail off with their herds as if they had gotten away with their thievery, then hit them from both sides with all they had.

The bandits were seemingly good at grouping the animals and began to head them back toward Victoria. After a couple of miles, Mr. Spillar fired his rifle into the air, which was a prearranged signal to attack. Tom told the boys to get after the rustlers with the horse herd and Spillar would attack the ones with the cattle. Before Jim knew what was happening, he was pursing the rustlers and firing his guns. He had to be careful as reloading with a cap and ball weapon on the back of Charlie was a seemingly impossible chore.

When they fired into the group, several fell out of their saddles, but Jim was not sure if he had hit anyone or not. Because of the surprise, no one was seriously injured from their group. One horse was shot and had to be destroyed later at the ranch. Mr. Spillar's group had the same type of good fortune with only one rider slightly wounded and one broken arm from a horse falling into a ditch. The bandits lost with five killed and eight to ten wounded. Mr. Spillar allowed them to carry off their dead and wounded but without his cattle and horses.

Jim was impressed with the professionalism exhibited during the skirmish.

"We were all a little afraid but doing the job with that fear is the mark of a brave man," Tom replied.

This saying stayed with Jim and had a dramatic impact on his life. Jim thought to himself, *I thought I was the only one terrified. I'm not that much different from the rest of the cowhands.* For the first time, he finally felt he was a member of the group.

He rode back to the ranch feeling good about his accomplishments, but a little sad when he realized he might have caused the death of another human being. He knew this was something he was going to have to get used to if he was going to ask Tom to assist him in becoming a Texas Ranger.

THE TEHUACANA BATTLE

Tom and Jim were branding cattle the next week when Jim got a surprise out of the blue.

"You handled yourself pretty good during the Mexican raid last week," Tom told Jim. "We were wondering if you would like to do a scout with a few rangers over near Tehuacana. There has been some Indian activity in the area with three farmers slain last week."

Jim was both floored and pleasantly surprised by the invitation.

"We were thinking about riding over tomorrow morning if they can finish with the branding this afternoon. Mr. Spillar can't go with us, but he agrees that something has to be done," Tom explained.

Jim didn't sleep much that night after putting Charlie in the corral. Jim did not ride Charlie every day as the rigors of ranch life were difficult on a cow pony. He had a string of mustangs furnished by the ranch that he used for everyday work. But when he had something that needed dependability, he always called on Charlie.

He stayed up late that night cleaning and oiling his weapons, two cap and ball revolvers and a double barrel break open shotgun. Jim had been hearing about a new pistol manufactured by Samuel Colt which fired six bullets but did not require loading the powder and projectile separately. It was all in one cartridge. Sam Colt was said to have made it based on the design of Ben McCulloch, the top Texas Ranger at the time. You could load it on Sunday and shoot it all week. Jim *thought I'll have a gun like that when I become a fulltime Texas Ranger.* The statement was made using when, not if, as Jim had gained a considerable amount of confidence following the conflict with the Mexican Raiders.

Early the next morning they rode out of the corral heading in a northwesterly direction toward the small settlement of Tehuacana. There were five from the ranch and another six on the edge of Mexia. The number of Indians to be confronted varied, depending on whom you talked to and the number ranged from ten to thirty braes. The thing that concerned Tom was why would they remain in that area for such an extended period of time. As they rode out of Mexia, Tom stressed that they be exceedingly careful as something did not seem right. Usually, the Indians raided and ran, but this time they were seemingly in no hurry to leave. There had been three deaths they knew of and possibly more by that time.

The community was approximately ten miles from Mexia with terrain consisting of lush grass with clusters and cottonwood and oak trees. The trees were thick enough to conceal several men until you were upon them. Tom's instructions to be exceedingly careful were foremost in Jim's mind.

"Hold up, I've got something to say!" Tom called out to the group once they were about five miles out of Mexia. The men reined up around the ranger.

"I'm still anxious about these Indians and what they are doing in the settlement for so long. I think we should send a couple of Rangers down to scout the area. Any volunteers?" Tom asked.

Without thinking, Jim volunteered. Tom was hesitant to accept him as a scout because of his age and lack of experience.

"Next time, Jim," Tom answered.

Bill Smith and Jake McCord volunteered and were readily accepted. They were instructed to hightail it back and report as soon as any contact or sighting was made.

Jake McCord was one of the rangers joining the scout just outside of Mexia. He was, comparably speaking, an older gentleman and, according to Tom, one of the lucky few that had escaped the carnage inflicted on the four hundred Texans at Goliad. He had also been with Sam Houston at the Battle of San Jacinto. He was asked to accompany Bill Smith to patrol the area in front of the main force. He readily agreed.

The scouts positioned themselves in the tree lines on opposite sides of the prairie, roughly one-half to three-quarters of a mile in front of the main body of rangers. The distance varied depending on the topography. They kept within the tree lines to conceal themselves from the

Indians. Jim could follow the scout because he pretty much knew where they were.

Along about noon, the scouts came back with an astonishing report. They had snuck in from the north and entered the small community unnoticed. The local citizens had been locked within the church. There were seven or eight wagons loaded with guns, ammunition, black powder, military weapons and supplies located within the Village Square. After they had searched the area as carefully as was deemed practical, Jake whispered to Bill Smith, his fellow scout, that they had better get back and relay the information to Tom Green. On their first few miles from the settlement, the scouts moved slowly, with caution, to avoid detection. When they reasoned they had enough distance between them, they used their spurs to quickly get back to the main body of men.

When they rode up to the main body of rangers, Jake and Bill hurriedly sought out Tom Green and told him what they had discovered.

"There appears to be a group of Indians, probably around thirty, and a Comancheros wagon train," Jake excitedly told Tom.

"I have never known of the Comancheros to be this far east. They stay pretty close to the Llano Estacado on the high plains of West Texas," Tom answered.

"I agree, but that's what it appears to be," Jake stated.

Tom called for a cold camp with sentries posted. He then held a meeting to inform the men what lay ahead. The men gathered around and listened intently to Tom's plan. Tom counted heads with eleven men present including the two rangers who had just returned from their reconnaissance.

"Men, they have what looks like a force of up to thirty Comanche braves and a Comancheros wagon train," the ranger captain said with conviction. "It appears the wagons are loaded with munitions and they ain't looking to hold a Sunday prayer meeting."

Jake spoke up and asked if it could be Northern agitators stirring up and arming Northern sympathizers.

Most of the local people were aware of the war clouds churning over the nation, but felt that was in the Northeast, not in Texas. Tom told the men not to discount the possibility, but it didn't really matter if it was Comancheros, Northern agitators, or some other type of menace. They had to protect their settlements and their citizens.

"I want you to go back to the ranch and get as many of the ranch hands as possible," Tom told Jim after calling him off to one side. "Explain to Mr. Spillar the gravity of the situation and the need for more guns. My plan is to attack from head on with flanking attacks from each side. To do this, we have to have more men."

"I plan to attack early tomorrow morning after what I hope is a night of heavy drinking and celebration on their part," Tom continued.

"It appeared whiskey was plentiful from what they could see," Jake said.

Jim rode hard back to Mexia and the ranch. Mrs. Spillar met him at the door and Jim asked if he could talk to Mr. Spillar. She said he was at the barn and he could find him there.

Spillar was talking to a couple of ranch hands when Jim rode up. Upon approach, Jim explained the situation and Mr. Spillar understood the gravity of the matter immediately.

"How many men does Tom need?" Mr. Spillar wanted to know.

"He told me ten, but from what I understood about the numbers they would be facing, they would still be outnumbered with that many," Jim replied.

In barely an hour, there were twelve men, including Mr. Spillar, with saddled horses and armed to the teeth. Mr. Spillar said goodbye to his wife and told her he would in all likelihood see her the next afternoon. He kissed her on the forehead, mounted his horse, and rode off with his men toward Tehuacana.

Jim thought to himself, I'm getting to be an old hand at this rangering business. He was a bit jittery, though, and wondered if he was the only one that was a little nervous.

When they got back to the cold camp later that afternoon, Tom brought Mr. Spillar up to date on the situation. He seemed to be pleased to share the burden of command with the big boss. Most of the men had a pretty good idea of what was being played out. They spent the rest of the afternoon cleaning their weapons, making sure they had plenty of ammunition, playing cards and mumble peg. Most of these rangers were just kids who had grown up quickly, maybe too quickly. They were still children in years lived, but each had to grow up before his time, committing gruesome deeds necessary to perform as frontier rangers.

The night was dark with the clouds covering the moon. No fires were permitted due to the possibility of warning the outlaws. Jim had no idea how much sleep the other men got, but he got very little. It was cold but not unbearable. He wondered what his family was doing back in Mississippi and if he would ever see them again. He finally dozed off seemingly about the time Tom shook him and told him he was ready to ride. The attack force was leaving in about twenty minutes. Jim had left his saddle on Charlie but the cinch straps were loose and the bridle's bits were unsnapped, hanging on the outside of her mouth to keep from grating her mouth. Charlie would stand over Jim while he slept, with the bridle reins usually on his chest or in close proximity. If something disturbing occurred the horse would nudge Jim until he was awake.

5

THE ATTACK

After a few hours of unrestful sleep, the time for the men to make their move came quickly. They hurriedly checked their weapons, mounted their horses, and waited for their orders. Tom divided the group into three fractions with him in charge of the frontal attack force and Jake and Mr. Spillar commanding the flanking groups.

The men were very surprised there were no pickets (enemy guards posted) on the outskirts of the camp. The force was divided up approximately one mile from the settlement with the two flanking movements angling off to each side. Tom would attack the larger force with a frontal assault. Due to the fact that no pickets were posted, the forces were able to station themselves in close proximity to the foe. The signal to attack was again, as it was with attacking the rustlers, a shot fired by Tom.

The shot was fired and the attack began just as the sun was coming up in the east. Even though the rangers were ready, it was a surprise when the shots rang out. They rode swiftly to the center of the settlement picking their targets as they went. The Indians were disoriented and, as hoped, were suffering from a case of drinking too much the night before. Several were killed and the rest ran away on their horses. Some attempted to surrender but died in the attempt. The rangers were not overly sympathetic after suffering years of atrocities on the frontier. The Comancheros were all captured and turned out to be natives of New York. Their mission was, as speculated earlier, to agitate and arm anyone who was an enemy of the South. They were blue-bellied Yankees. Their wagon loads of munitions were seized and taken back to Mexia for storage. What to do with the Yankees was a dilemma. The general consensus among the Rangers was to shoot them. They were considered to be traitors or spies and, in most cases, would ordinarily be condemned to the firing squads. When the time came, Tom took them back to Mexia and turned them over to the sheriff who placed them in the local jail.

The local citizens were released from their confinement in the church with much gratitude demonstrated. No one was injured by the Indians or their Comancheros friends from the North. By 10:00 a.m., the situation had come under control with Mr. Spillar and Tom gathering up his rangers and appointing the local constable to organize the local citizens and dispose of the dead after the rangers left.

The town folks agreed to dispose of the Indian bodies by burning their corpses in a big bonfire, but only after scalping each one. The rangers had suffered no injuries due largely to the complete surprise and the tactics of the attack. The strategy utilized, a frontal assault with synchronized attacks on the flanks, would be made famous by General

Nathan Bedford Forrest in the coming war between the States.

The group of rangers rode back to Mexia with a feeling that was not of joy but of having done something that was necessary to maintain safety and well-being for people on the frontier. The prisoners had been interrogated and readily admitted that a civil war was a foregone conclusion and they were here to create mayhem amid what they considered enemy territory.

Not long ago, Jim and his cousin Billy Roy had heard rumblings about the war but did not pay a lot of attention to it. Like many others around them, they were cowboys and rangers who did not pay a lot of attention to politics and hardly ever read a newspaper. This conflict with the Comancheros, however, brought the problem front and center. Jim heard the next week that the 10th Texas infantry was recruiting a company over in Fairfield, a settlement about twenty miles to the east. He and some of the boys thought they would ride over and see what this was all about.

Jim was not quite seventeen at the time and his family, nor anyone they knew, for that matter, owned a slave. It was just the idea that someone from up North could dictate how the people in the South should live that bothered him. At any rate, he guessed the war would probably be over before they ever saw any action. Even if it did come to blows, it was felt that one southern country boy would be able to whip ten northern city boys in a fair fight.

Of course, as Jim and his southern friends would determine in a relatively short period of time, fighting the industrialized north would not be fair. It would not take long to realize that the northern boys were not soft and made excellent soldiers. Jim and his friends, however, were young and had proven themselves fighting local outlaws and Indians. They wanted to go off on the great adventure and fight for their country.

6

GOING TO WAR

Monday morning Jim and six other young cowboys rode over to Fairfield to see what the recruiter had to say about the 10th Texas. The person attempting to enlist the new recruits was the town mayor, a Mr. Price. He was appointed as a Lt. Colonel of Volunteers. He promised adventure and glory to all who signed up, but they were going to train hard and go right into battle. The plan was to leave Fairfield by the end of the week.

Almost all the guys in the units were from local ranches and personally knew each other. A lot of these boys were brothers, cousins, or had been friends for a long time. Everyone was concerned that the war would be over before they could get there. Jim told Colonel Price that he had to go back to the Spillar Ranch to wind up some business, but he would be back before the end of the week.

Jim's trip back to Mexia was a mixture of sadness and excitement. He was sad about leaving the ranch where he had made so many friends and hated to part from a family that had been so good to him. He considered Mr.

and Mrs. Spillar surrogate parents and loved them dearly. He was excited, though, about becoming a member of the Confederate Military, too.

He arrived back in Fairfield and explained to Mr. and Mrs. Spillar how much they meant to him but he felt that it was his patriotic duty to join the army and fight for his country. The Spillars were saddened but understood. Jim arrived back at Fairfield and reported straight away to Colonel Price. The Colonel immediately administered the oath and, just like that, he was Private James Jefferson Walker. He was assigned to the rifle squad as a rifleman. His weapon was a 0.58 caliber musket that had a bayonet fixture on the end. The first weeks were spent learning military drills and more drills. Jim was not sure there was anyone present who really had a background in the military.

The mayor was not a professional soldier, but he had spent some time in the Mexican war and with the Rangers. He seemed to know what he was doing, but they couldn't know for sure as they had no experience in these areas. They left the Fairfield area on Saturday morning and went for additional training in the East Texas piney woods near St. Augustine. The troops stayed there for approximately six weeks with the new troopers arriving every day. Each trooper was issued Confederate uniforms, rifles, and all accruements necessary to go to war. They were also issued one half of a pup tent where two soldiers would have to partner up to have a complete shelter. A great deal of time was spent marching and performing other kinds of military drills. They figured that if marching could win a war, they would be undefeated.

The recruits spent a lot of time speculating about when they were going to move and where they would be going. One of the boys from Centreville was bitten by a coral snake one night. There was little anyone could do to help him. By the time they discovered him, the venom was far too advanced to save his life. It was sad to see a young man in the prime of his youth, dying in front of them with no power to save him. They buried him the next morning with the unit's chaplain conducting the funeral. It was the first of countless deaths they were to encounter over the next few years. The lucky one would be buried with Christian words read over them. Most, however, would be left in the open with the elements. Notwithstanding, the new troopers were getting antsy. They were ready to meet the enemy.

Jim became reunited with a boy with whom he had worked closely on the Spillar Ranch. They became close since they had joined the unit together and had been assigned to the same rifle squad. His name was Robert Johnson, but everyone called him Bobby. Bobby was eighteen and had been born in West Columbia about twenty miles west of Angleton. He was an outstanding cowboy, a good bronc rider, and he could read and write fluently. The ability to read and write was unusual in that day in early Texas as the school systems were not advanced. Most kids were home-schooled if they were fortunate to have literate parents.

One night while sitting around the campfire before taps, Bobby asked Jim if he thought he could kill someone he did not know. Jim told him he thought he had and related his experiences with the Mexican Bandits and the Indians at Tehuacana. He had not, however, killed someone who was up close and personal. He added that he had always fired into a group with others firing at the same time. In that environment, nobody knew whose bullet had done the damage. Jim told him that was good as far as he was concerned. Bobby replied that killing someone he didn't know who was only there because he had been directed to do so didn't bother him. Jim thought to himself *Bobby is very mature and seems to have a lot of wisdom for his age.*

They woke up the next morning, which was a Sunday, and attended a church service conducted by the chaplain who was a Catholic priest. Jim had been raised in the Baptist church, but he felt that organized religion had little to do with one's relationship with God. Jim's concept of religion was that God should be exalted and his fellow man should be treated with dignity and respect. If someone didn't follow those tenants, he figured they would have a hard time being a Christian. And so, it didn't matter to Jim the denomination of the minister so long as he could worship the Lord.

After the service and lunch, Colonel Price called a meeting of the troopers in the 10th Texas to be held at the parade ground. While there, the colonel stated that they had been at the site for six weeks, though he knew it seemed it had been much longer. He also said he hoped they had absorbed enough tactics to give them a fighting chance. The next morning, they were to move out following their first formation. The unit gave an enthusiastic cheer in response as everyone was anxious to leave the encampment.

That evening, before dark, Jim and Bobby went to pay respects at the freshly covered grave of the boy from Centerville for the last time. They felt sad, having experienced the first of what would be many tragic deaths together.

7

ON THE MARCH

After reveille and breakfast the next morning, they strapped on their packs, placed their muskets on their shoulders and marched out of camp to their next destination. They marched east toward the Sabine River, which was the boundary between Texas and Louisiana. The trip across the river was done by ferry. The exorbitant charge for crossing the river caused them to believe the ferry operator was more gracious to Yankees than he was to their forces.

They encamped again for a couple of days with rumors rampant. They were going to Virginia to join General Robert E. Lee, then would join General Joseph E. Johnson in Georgia, and then, finally, march northeast through Louisiana and join Albert Sidney Johnson and his interdiction of the North's General Grant and General Buell at a place on the Tennessee River called Pittsburgh Landing or, as the South called it, Shiloh.

The unit left camp and marched from the small hamlet of Nacogdoches, Texas to Mansfield, Louisiana, to Monroe, Louisiana and crossed the big Mississippi river at Vicksburg.

The Southern people on the way treated them like heroes, but Vicksburg was the most patriotic city of all. It was difficult going through the city with all the temptations of food, drink, pretty girls, and more everywhere around them. Little did they know the 10th would be in a life and death struggle in the greater Vicksburg area in the not-too-distant future.

After finally leaving the city behind them, they headed for the settlement of Starkville and on to Corinth, Mississippi where they would join up with General Albert Sidney Johnston and march with him on to meet General Grant at Pittsburgh Landing in Tennessee.

After a week of hard marching, the troops entered Corinth, Mississippi and were startled by what they saw. It seemed all the buildings in the town, including private residences, had been transformed into hospitals. It seemed there had already been a battle there that they had missed.

Bobby asked a Corporal Jones of the 1st Mississippi what happened. The Colonel explained that they had met Grant at Shiloh Church just over the Tennessee state line on April 6th. Though they had whipped the northern army pretty good, they did not follow up and Southern generals instead allowed their troops to encamp with complete victory to be completed the next day.

During the night, however, General Buell of the north arrived and disembarked with ten thousand Yankee troops which enabled Grant's forces to rout the Confederates the second day. It was then that the south lost General Johnston, one of the best generals on either side of the war, during the Battle of the Hornet's Nest.

Corporal Jones' tale of woe continued, stating that the Southern army, recognizing it was hopeless, gathered its forces and headed back south toward Corinth. It had started to rain with the wagons creating big ruts in the road and the wounded crying out in agony and pain. The whole Confederate Army of the West would have been lost except for Colonel Bedford Forrest who fought a rear-guard action against General Sherman of "March Across Georgia" fame.

General Forrest was severely wounded during this action at the small hamlet of Monterey, but he did enable the defeated army to make it back to Corinth, Mississippi, to regroup and to fight again. Some things became clear to Jim and his fellow troopers: the war would not be a short one and the glory would not outshine the true horrors of the conflict.

These mutilated kids were close to Jim's age and had horrific wounds on their bodies. The glory was quickly recognized as superficial and patriotism was taking a backseat to common sense. These kid soldiers with shattered bodies didn't own a plantation or slaves or other accruements of the landed gentry. He remembered what Tom had said before he left for Fairfield to join the military: "It's a rich man's war and a poor man's fight."

Life is just not fair, he thought to himself. One of the things that Jim was beginning to be aware of that was necessary for growing up was to recognize the fact that life was not always fair.

The 10th Texas stayed at Corinth for about a month helping to fortify the area for Grant's attack which everyone knew was just a matter of time. But the large-scale assault expected never materialized. At the end of the month they were ordered to pack up and be ready to march again on quick notice. Where? No one seemed to know.

When the orders came to march, they were headed south toward what each thought was the road to Vicksburg. The rumors were widespread that they would be reinforcing General Pemberton's command at Vicksburg which was regarded by the Confederates as the "Gibraltar of the West. There were 33,000 troopers, including some navy men, under Pemberton's command. They marched south by southwest going through Oxford, the future site of the University of Mississippi, and instead of continuing their southward course, they almost turned due west. They crossed the Tallahatchie river by boat and marched west again through the Mississippi delta until they came to the mouth of the Arkansas river where it emptied into the Mississippi river.

The 10th Texas then crossed to the Arkansas side by boat and set up their tents until all the units were across. Jim and Bobby gathered wood for a campfire and cooked their rations completely unaware what their next move would be. The platoon sergeant called them together and told them to set up their tents as they would spend the night there. Tomorrow, he told them, they would be marching to Fort Hindman or, as it had been more commonly known, the Arkansas Post. The stronghold was named after Confederate General Thomas C. Hindman of Arkansas. The location had been constructed on a bluff twenty-five feet above the north side of the river and forty-five miles downriver from Pine Bluff. The unit would fortify the Arkansas River from northern incursions against the cities of Pine Bluff and Little Rock.

8

ARKANSAS POST

The Arkansas Post was manned after the arrival of the 10th Texas with roughly 5,500 men, primarily Texas Cavalry, dismounted and redeployed as infantry. The force consisted of three brigades under the command of Brigadier General Thomas J. Churchill. By the winter of 1862-63, disease and their position at the end of shaky supply chain had left the garrison in a poor state. The base also served as a foundation for disrupting shipping on the Mississippi river and provided support for Vicksburg.

One evening, the sergeant told the platoon to get a good night's sleep and be ready to move out after reveille the next morning. Jim and Bobby just looked at each other in some degree of bewilderment and crawled into their sleeping bags.

The next morning the 10th Texas moved out on the northern side of the Arkansas river through country that was completely new to the troopers.

The new area was strange to the country boys and to some degree was treated as a new adventure for them all.

Jim had not traveled much in his short life, but it seemed he had traveled more than anyone else in his unit. The sun was sinking in the west when they saw the salient of Arkansas Post. They camped for the night on the outside of the fort. They could, and would, become permanent residents the next day.

The time period following their arrival at the fort to the time of the battle was spent in building ramparts, primarily gun emplacement and rifle pits. There was a lot of boredom and rumors spread primarily about the Yankee's movement against Vicksburg. A lot of time was spent digging rifle pits which provided a view of the river for approximately one mile in both directions. There were posted sentinels but the troopers themselves also kept a keen eye peeled for possibly enemy forces moving up or down the river. Jim and Bobby were expecting company in the form of blue-clad troopers coming from the east at any time.

Jim missed his best friend Charlie. The 10th was a Texas cavalry unit, but they were deployed as a dismounted infantry unit. Jim had been forced to leave Charlie at the ranch in Mexia. It was good thing because it might have been difficult to feed her. Food was scarce for the troopers with very little, and sometimes none, for the animals. The grass was almost bare during the fall and winter months.

The lack of adequate supplies on a weak supply line contributed to malnutrition. This resulted in several cases of childhood diseases which proved deadly for many. Several of the fellow troopers in Jim's unit succumbed during their encampment at Arkansas Post. It was a sad that the young men, who were away from home for the first time, died without family nearby to comfort them. The winter was hard, too, with much ice and snow, but the protection provided by the fort's living quarters proved to be adequate.

After a month of boredom, Jim and Bobby were sitting on the ramparts when they saw several large boats approaching from the east. They sat on the wooden planks and stared until they realized the boats meant they were being invaded by Northern troops. Jim and Bobby ran to the supply hut and were issued as much shot and powder as they could carry and lodged themselves in one of the rifle pits nearby. The feelings turned from absolute boredom to excitement and a little bit fearful, too. Bobby commented to Jim, "Man, there are a lot of blue troopers on those boats."

There were a lot of enemy in the force coming up the river. Union Major General John A. McClernand, a politician who had secured a military appointment from President Lincoln had arrived with an army-sized offensive consisting of approximately 33,000 soldiers and sailors. McClernand was short on military training but long on political ambition. He had deceitfully gained his military force for an offensive against Vicksburg. He called his 33,000 man force the Army of the Mississippi and without the permission or knowledge of either President Lincoln or the overall commander at Vicksburg, General Grant, he launched the offensive against Arkansas Post hoping for glory and political gain. He also ordered Grant's right hand man, Major General Sherman, to join his forces as his second in command without Grant's permission as well.

On January 9ᵗʰ, the force started up the river toward the fort with Sherman corps overrunning the Confederate trenches. Bobby and Jim retreated behind the protective wall of the fort. The Navy under Flag Officer David Porter, on January 10ᵗʰ moved his gunboats towards the fort and opened a bombardment. Jim and Bobby peered out from the slits in the rifle pits as the fleet sailed past the fort effectively cutting off any thought of retreat or resupply. The shelling from the ironclads and the Yankee artillery on the south side of the river in point of fact suppressed the fort's big guns. This envelopment caused General Churchill to turn over his sword to McClernand that afternoon despite the orders to defend the fort at all costs.

The casualties were relatively light if you were not one of them. Of the 5,500 Confederates at the fort, 4,791 surrendered. A number of the rebels in the outer perimeter of the defensive line simply climbed out of their rifle pits, walked into the woods and escaped. Jim and Bobby and most of their unit were not so lucky. Their rifle pit was on the interior of the defensive line and they had nowhere to go. They had no choice but to throw down their muskets and surrender.

"I've never surrendered before and it's scary, shameful, and disgraceful. At least that's the way I feel," Bobby told Jim with tears running down his cheeks.

A Yankee three stripper, or buck sergeant, arrived and addressed their unit.

"Take all of your military accruements and put it in a pile in front of your ranks. Keep your canteens and shelter halves. After you have piled your equipment as directed, just sit down in place until you they know where you'll be going," the buck sergeant commanded.

"Where will we be going?" One of the fellows asked.

"I don't know for sure, but I expect some of the troopers will be going to Camp Douglas in Chicago and some will end up in Camp Chase in Columbus, Ohio," the sergeant answered.

They were fed in the middle of the afternoon. It was the first decent meal they had eaten in months. They even had seconds if they wanted them and everyone did.

The prisoners were issued blankets since it was January and the nights were cold. The next morning, they got up at six and were fed a hearty breakfast.

"Why do you think all those steam ships or paddle wheelers are lined up in the river?" Bobby asked Jim.

"That is probably our transportation to our new residence in Chicago or Columbus," Jim replied with a look of resignation and despondency on his face. "It is so hard to accept our surrender. I think I'd have rather died fighting."

Shortly thereafter, they were called to attention and placed in columns of deuces, or twos, and marched down to the landing wharf. They were marched onto the paddle wheelers to begin their journey to the prison camps. Jim and Bobby had the good fortune to be placed on the same boat. However, it was very crowded. Finding their own place to eat and sleep was a nightmare.

Of course, Jim did not know that the Yankees suffered a total of 1,047 casualties, either killed or wounded. The Confederates suffered almost their entire force as casualties who constituted their total contingent, almost all by surrender, except the ones who slipped away before and during their capitulation. It constituted one of the largest surrenders of Confederate troops west of the Mississippi river prior to the end of the war in 1865.

Jim, with his friends and fellow soldiers, sat onboard their ship all that day and into the night. They finally got started about two hours after the sun had finally dipped below the small hills to the west. Rumors were rampant on where their destination would be. They even gambled on to which prison camp they were going. The Yankees didn't seem to mind as they were using confederate currency. The money was worth nothing in the north and not much more in the south. Approximately two hours after they started, they came to the mouth of the Arkansas river where it emptied into the Mississippi river. The boat turned north, but that did not solve the mystery of whether they were headed toward Camp Douglas in Illinois or Camp Chase in Ohio. Only time would tell.

9

THE ESCAPE

Jim nudged Bobby the first morning on the big river and asked him, "Do you notice anything?"

"What am I looking for?" Bobby asked with a puzzled look on his face.

"See how close the boat comes to shore from time to time?" Jim replied.

"I haven't been paying any attention," Bobby answered.

"I hope the guards haven't been paying much attention either. Can you swim?" Jim asked, thinking they might have found a way to escape.

"Yes, I can," Bobby replied.

"When the ship comes closer to the shore, I think if we could work our way to the edge of the boat, without causing suspicion, we might have a chance to jump overboard and swim to shore," Jim explained.

For the rest of the day, Jim and Bobby worked to maneuver themselves closer and closer to the outside railing. At about four in the afternoon, they heard a lot of shouting coming from the mid-section of the ship. Evidently, some of the others onboard had a similar idea and had jumped overboard as a group. It was carnage as the guards shot the prisoners as they attempted to swim to shore.

"I'm glad we didn't just try that," Bobby said, with a look of terror on his face. "It was nothing but suicide."

"Not so fast," Jim replied. "I think it can be done. Have you ever noticed the trees and other debris floating down the river, especially near the shore? We could time our escape to jump in the water and use those trees to shield our bodies from the rifle fire. The ship is traveling north going against the river's current and the trees are being swept downstream by the current. If we can jump behind one of those logs and keep low, we can be out of range of the rifles in a short period of time."

Another consideration was that the farther they traveled north on the river, the longer they would have to spend in enemy territory.

Later that evening, as the sun set in the west, the ship veered toward the western bank of the river to avoid a sandbar. Bobby and Jim couldn't help noticing a lot of limbless trees and tree stumps, which looked as if they came from a logging operation.

"I don't really want to do this," Jim whispered, "but this is probably the best opportunity we're going to get to escape."

"I agree," Bobby agreed. "Let's go!"

At that moment, each boy placed their hands on the railing and vaulted themselves into the Mississippi, hoping to hit nothing but water when they landed. Once in the water, they hurriedly ducked their heads beneath the surface and reemerged behind a large floating log. From the boat, the boys heard what seemed like every guard shooting and they became concerned about the log coming apart. After about ten minutes, the distance finally made good aim difficult from the boat, but they could still hear rifle fire coming from behind them. The shots were coming from a boat to the rear of the other. They had to shift their positions quickly to avoid the bullets coming from the other boat.

After the ships got past a sandbar, they steered out into the middle of the river leaving the boys to their own devices. In the dark, they paddled their tree, which had saved their lives, to a small inlet where they could wade onto the riverbank.

The boys were wet and cold. It was the middle of the January and it was beginning to rain.

To stay warm and dry, they found a protective cove on the river to shelter them from the rain and wind. They laid close to each other so they could stay warm. Exhausted, they slept until they heard a rooster crowing from a nearby farm. They had no idea where they were except somewhere on the western bank of the Mississippi river. Jim estimated they were mostly likely in northern Arkansas or southern Missouri.

"If we're lucky," Jim told Bobby, "we're in an area that is sympathetic to the southern cause. There some real bad people in Missouri that have no love for us or what we stand for."

After another night's sleep, they realized they looked a mess. Their clothes were wet and muddy. They had not shaved or conducted any personal hygiene since the morning the fort capitulated and not much for the two days prior to that. They were not hungry, but they would be soon. None of this mattered to the boys, though. They were glad to be alive.

Jim and Bobby knew their next step was to determine where they were and how to get home without being shot. They knew their military unit did not exist anymore. It was destroyed at the Arkansas Post and there was no longer anyone there to whom they could report. Jim' plan was to get back to Mexia and reorganize.

Bobby was from West Columbia, Texas, a town about two hundred miles south of Mexia. Desperate for a job, he had ridden up to the Spillar Ranch when he heard they were hiring. His main thought was returning to West Columbia.

Jim looked at him and asked what he thought their next move should be.

"What do I want to do next?" Bobby replied with excitement. "I want to go home!"

Jim reminded him that they could be in enemy country and he needed to hold his voice down. Bobby said he got so worked up about going home that he could not help almost shouting.

Despite the fact they were dirty, hungry, and lost, they were euphoric to be alive and free.

Jim knew the Mississippi ran north and south and the boat was going north. He also figured they were on the west side of the boat and, knowing that, they knew which direction to head to reach friendly territory.

They had seen some semblance of smoke off in the distance, so they knew a settlement was near. They just didn't know if it was friendly or not. They also had to be careful because they could be mistaken for deserters and shot without an opportunity to explain.

At this time, there were a lot of Confederate troops becoming disheartened with the war who simply went home. Most of the troops in the ranks owned no slaves or a had a plantation to protect. They had gone to war over a conflict that could have been over before they arrived on the battlefield. The epigram most often quote after years of privations and seeing their friends slaughtered hardened their hearts and they concluded it was a rich man's war and a poor man's fight.

Jim looked at Bobby and said, "Let's go over to the settlement and see if we can see if we can find someone who might be willing to help us."

The settlement was about two miles west of the river. After about a mile, they came upon a relatively well-maintained ranch and dairy farm with a large herd of Holstein cattle and several horses.

"Do you think we should approach these people or go into the village?" Jim asked Bobby.

"I think we'll probably have better luck with the country folks than the city persons," Bobby answered.

"I agree," Jim said as he walked up to an older man coming out of the milking barn.

"Good morning, sir," Jim said to the man. "We are Confederate soldiers who escaped from a steam ship taking us, to the best of our knowledge, to a prison camp in Chicago."

The man looked them over carefully, listening closely to Jim's story.

"We were captured at Arkansas Post a few days ago," Jim continued. "We don't know exactly where we are or if this is a Confederate or northern territory. We were with the Tenth Texas Dismounted Cavalry out of Fairfield, Texas. We are trying to get back to Texas and home."

The man nodded as Jim looked him square in the eye and said, "We are putting our lives in your hands without knowing where your loyalties lie."

Stepping back, the man replied, "My name is Thomas Weatherby and my loyalties are with neither side. We have tried to remain neutral and, so far, we've been fortunate. Some of the neighboring farms and small settlements have been attacked by the likes of Cantrell or Bloody Bill Anderson's bands of cutthroats. We've been left pretty much alone by the Missouri Redlegs and Kansas Jayhawkers."

Jim and Bobby each breathed a sigh of relief as the old man continued.

"The Yankees and Confederates have been so busy with Vicksburg we don't see much of either side. It appears to me what you really need is a bath, clean clothes, and a meal. We'll worry about getting you back to Texas after we take care of these necessities."

Mr. Weatherby told them he had a couple of boys around their age who he wanted to keep out of the horrible war.

Jim and Bobby could not believe their good fortune and followed Mr. Weatherby like two puppy dogs to the barn and stock watering trough. The trough was about three feet high and about ten feet across. He told them they could take a bath there.

"Don't worry," Mr. Weatherby laughed. "There are no girls here at the barn, so don't be embarrassed. While you two get washed up, I will see if I can find some decent clothes for you to wear. I think my sons' clothes will fit y'all as you appear to be about the same sizes."

The boys bathed and were happy to finally have an opportunity to clean up. The excitement of being free and happening onto Mr. Weatherby was mind-boggling.

Jim and Bobby had a long way to get back to Texas, but a big hurdle had been cleared.

Mr. Weatherby soon arrived with clean clothes and even socks. They had not had socks since they were at Spillar Ranch. The clothes were somewhat loose, but that was mostly due to the boys' lack of nutrition over the past year. Regardless, they felt really good.

Mr. Weatherby took them to the main house and introduced them to his family, including his three daughters and two sons, whose clothes they were wearing. They never asked if the boys were twins, but they appeared to be as they looked alike and were around the same age. Mr. Weatherby had evidently already explained the boys' plight since everybody was being so nice to them. They were seated along a long table with the center filled with wonderful food in bowls, large platters of hot cornbread and biscuits, rolls complete with butter and big glasses of iced tea or sweet milk, whatever their preference. After dinner, there were different types of pie and it was wonderful. The boys had never had a meal so good, even at home or the Spillar Ranch.

Mr. Weatherby suggested they stay for a few days at the farm to rest up, gather their strength and figure out their route and method of getting home. He said there were facilities in the barn's tact room for them to stay. He added that it might look suspicious to visitors coming to the farm to see two trooper-aged boys, so staying in the barn was the best option.

Even so, the barn was a step up from what they were used to in the army. They had outdoor privy near the building with comfortable beds in the tact room itself. Bobby told Jim that based on the facilities there in the barn, he bet they weren't the first soldiers in trouble the Weatherbys had helped.

Though the barn had a distinctive smell of cow manure, neither boy minded. Having grown up on farms, it kind of reminded them of home. It is hard to explain to city people how such a seemingly offensive smell tends to make a country boy feel comfortable.

10

THE GUERILLA ATTACK

The first few days spent at the farm consisted mostly of eating and sleeping. They would help on the farm any way they could when there were no strangers around. They knew they had to be careful as there were neighboring folk with differing loyalties who might want to collect rewards for turning in deserters.

On the third day, Mr. Weatherby called a meeting with his family and the local sheriff present. The sheriff stated that they had captured a member of the Bloody Bill Anderson militia. When interrogating the captive, they learned that the militia was planning a raid in the vicinity to secure riding mounts and cattle for slaughter. They were a bloodthirsty bunch and were known to kill anyone in their path. The sheriff was concerned that they had set their sights on the Weatherby farm.

"We are not sure of the date or time, but we feel it might either be tonight or tomorrow night," the sheriff told them. "We will move all civilians, such as women and children, to other, safer, locations as soon as possible. I will place my militia in various buildings to give Mr. Anderson and his bloody bunch a proper welcome. We must start preparing right away, though. We don't have a lot of time."

"This is not your fight," Mr. Weatherby said, turning to Bobby and Jim. "You don't have to stay. You are free to leave now."

Jim looked at Bobby, who agreed without saying a word.

"No, sir," Jim replied. "Your fight is our fight, but we will need some guns. We lost our weapons at the surrender."

Mr. Weatherby nodded and put his hand on Jim' shoulder. He was proud to have such fine young men on his side.

The next few hours were spent moving the family and any other non-combatants out and preparing the home for the siege. The farmhouse was large and built to sustain harsh Midwest winters and devastating spring storms. It had wooden shutters with openings ideal for shooting a rifle through. With such a sturdy building to fight from, the group knew they had a good chance of beating the bloody bunch.

By five o'clock in the afternoon they were as ready as they were going to be. After the posse had taken their defensive positions, all they could do was wait.

The men that Mr. Weatherby had called together were very similar to the ones that Jim had known back in Mexia. They were men who led their lives in ordinary fashion but came together for common security. This philosophy of joining forces to protect the group had also been the genesis of the formation of the Texas Rangers.

Bobby and Jim took positions in the barn with several of the other men. They were friendly but nobody asked personal questions, which was good. Most of the group were local and held jobs such as farmers, merchants, and schoolteachers. Though there had been some time earlier in the day for idle conversation, now all talk was focused on the probable struggle before them.

Not being from the area, Jim and Bobby had never heard of Bloody Bill Anderson and were unsure what to expect. The locals told them he considered himself a military arm of the Confederate army, but he was just a bloodthirsty cutthroat who followed no rules of warfare. He was known to kill women and children without batting his eye. The Confederate army wanted nothing to do with this horrible man.

As time wore on and the moon shone from above, the men took turns serving as sentries posted around the farm to give advance warning of the enemy's approach. While not scouting, some of the men passed the time by playing poker and dominos.

During this time, Jim and Bobby stepped out of the barn and marveled at the beautiful night. Looking up at the full moon, they commented on how lucky they were to have the good visibility it offered of the surrounding area. It reminded Jim of nights back in Texas and what they called a Comanche moon. In the nights when the moon was like this, Comanches were known to make raids while they had the light such a moon provided.

Suddenly, Jim was jostled from his thoughts of home when Bobby tapped him eagerly on the shoulder.

"What is that movement on the prairie to the southwest?" Bobby asked as quietly as possible.

At that point, one of the lookouts came riding up to the house.

"They're coming! They're coming!" The sentry shouted.

"Take your places, men! It appears that our guests of honor have arrived!"

Mr. Weatherby hollered, stepping onto the porch with his weapon.

Mr. Weatherby had issued the boys Remington repeating rifles, which were new and astonishing to them. With such a weapon, it seemed that one man could hold off an attack of several by himself. Running into the main house, they found positions in windows where they had a wide range of fire.

Bloody Bill's militia was getting pretty close when one of the men in the house yelled, "That's Anderson's group! That's him out in front!"

"Let them have it, boys!" Mr. Weatherby shouted at the top of his lungs, causing the entire farm to erupt with shot and shell.

The first fusillade emptied many saddles and several horses received shotgun wounds as well. At that point, it appeared that Anderson was wounded but he managed to stay in his saddle and rode way. Despite this, it appeared that half of the attacking force had already been killed with several more wounded but able to escape.

Several of Weatherby's force attempted to grab their horses' reins and mount, but Mr. Weatherby restrained them from giving chase.

"They're beat," he told them. "Let them go off and lick their wounds. I doubt they'll be attacking anyone for a long time after so many losses."

After the battle, several saddled horses wandered around the farmhouse and barn. The unwelcome, dead intruders were loaded in the back of a horse drawn farm wagon and taken to the back of the property for burial in a mass grave. Mr. Weatherby directed the men to run the horses into the corral and shut the gate. He called Bobby and Jim over and told them to pick a couple for themselves. He knew riding those horses would beat attempting to reach Texas on foot.

The horses were highbred with excellent bridles and saddles, outfitted for men who made their living on horseback. Bobby picked a blaze-faced Sorrel and Jim singled out an Appaloosa, a rare but outstanding breed. Mr. Weatherby told them to check their mounts and see if everything was usable.

After the boys were done, Mr. Weatherby told them they were welcome to stay there as long as they wanted, but he understood if they wanted to get back to Texas and home. He just asked them to stay one more night, eat a good meal, and leave the next day. That would give him time to help them map out a route and furnish them with supplies for their journey.

The next day, Mr. Weatherby told them to keep their rifles and provided them with an abundance of ammunition taken from the fallen gunmen the night before. To travel hundreds of miles through possibly hostile territory without a weapon was nothing short of suicidal. The boys felt good to have their weapons, for protection and for food.

11

THE JOURNEY HOME

The journey home was tentatively mapped staring toward Little Rock and Shreveport before making the southward push from Dallas to Mexia. After thanking Mr. Weatherby and saying goodbye to his family, the boys with a good night's sleep and hearty breakfast on their side, began their southwestern ride toward Little Rock. Their hearts were heavy leaving the Weatherbys, but the thought of going home was exhilarating. Jim was concerned about having a new horse that might compete with Charlie, but the thought that weighed most on his mind was whether Charlie was alright and well-kept at the Spillar Ranch.

On their way, they rode close to towns to maintain direction, but skirted ranches and more populated areas. They knew it would be difficult to explain why they were not members of an organized military unit. Also, since the surrender of Arkansas Post, federal gunboats and Yankee military units were reaching as far west as Pine Bluff and Little Rock. To be on the safe side, the boys decided they would only travel at night until they covered the Red River back into Texas.

At about noon on the first day, the boys came across an abandoned shack with bunk beds and a cook stove. They couldn't believe their luck, but knew they had to be careful. They were afraid to start a fire for fear that someone might see the smoke. Though it appeared the shack had not been used in some time, so they felt relatively safe. Due to the excitement of the previous day, sleep came easily, and both were asleep by the time their heads rested on the crude beds.

When Jim awoke, Bobby was still sleeping peacefully. He shook him gently to rouse him from his slumber.

"What time is it?" Bobby asked.

"The sun is just starting to set in the west," Jim replied. "It's time to eat and start making our way to the Texas border.

After a cold supper, the boys saddled their horses and rode southwest with the full moon maintaining their direction. When they had almost ridden the entire night, they found a thicket of live oak trees where they could hide themselves and their horses. This was how they planned to hide during the daylight hours. Fortunately, they found fresh water to drink nearby along with grazing and a protective cove to feed and protect their horses.

When night fell again, they began their trek toward the Texas border. Despite their excitement, they knew they had to maintain a precautionary amount of calmness until they reached Mexia. Jim reminded Bobby that they must not only be careful of any Yankee or Confederate Militia, but also marauding Indians who might take advantage of the lack of a protective military guarding the frontier. Since the United States Cavalry had been removed to fight in a war between the states, some fighting for the Yankees, some for the Confederate, but none to protect the frontier from raids of any kind.

Even when the troops were stationed on the frontier, the Comanches were sure to come down from Fort Sill during the full moon once a month. These raids were usually concentrated on the outlying counties???? of Jack, Palo Pinto, Wise, and Parker. Prior to the Cavalry leaving, the Comanches did not venture east of these counties due to the high probability of being cut off from their escape route. With the military off fighting a war between themselves, this was no longer a threat.

Most of the raids were not for killing, but utilized for stealing stock, good horses in particular. The Indians were excellent judges of good horse flesh. In very rare cases, they would steal children to raise for their own or trade them back to their families for a profit. One of these children was 10-year-old Cynthia Ann Parker, abducted during a raid on Fort Parker near Groesbeck, Texas, and raised as a Comanche until she reached adulthood and married Chief Nocona, with whom she raised a family. She was eventually recaptured and returned to her birth family at the age of 34. After ten years of heartache over being separated from the Comanche and losing her daughter to pneumonia, Cynthia Ann died of self-inflicted starvation in 1871.

12

THE INDIAN RAIDS

Just a little over two days into their journey, the boys met a train of six wagons coming straight toward them. Before they started to veer away from the trail, Bobby stopped Jim.

"Let's see where they are going in those ox-pulled wagons." Bobby said, riding toward the group.

Just then, two men separated from the others and began to ride hard toward Bobby and Jim.

"Who are you and where are you going?" Bobby shouted to them.

"We're heading to far east Texas to avoid a large band of Indians who jumped the reservation and were plundering and killing everyone!" The man shouted back excitedly.

Slowing down, the two riders explained they were up from Denton county after confronting a large band of one thousand Indians or maybe more, mostly thought to be from the Comanche and Kiowa tribes.

It had been a killing raid with farms and ranches plundered, women raped, and one and all killed before moving on. A large group of settlers, the men said, had barricaded themselves at forts Richardson and Belknap, northwest of Weatherford, Texas, and were managing to survive. It seemed the only people who survived the raid were those who secured themselves in ranch houses with large groups of neighbors. As the settlers hoped, the Indians generally bypassed their strongholds for easier pickings.

The men asked Bobby and Jim if they would like to go with them until it was safer to travel.

"No," Jim told the man. "We plan to travel mostly at night in hopes that Mexia is south of the Indians' present path."

The men warned the boys not to travel north or west – just to turn south as quickly as possible. They told the boys they thought riding at night was a good idea.

"How far is it to Mexia?" One of the men asked.

"I'm not exactly sure," Jim answered. "I figure we've got about 300 more miles to go."

The man nodded and wished the boys well.

With that, Bobby and Jim spurred their mounts and headed east with a little bit of fear within them.

After riding as hard as they could, keeping only their destination and possibility of attack on their mind, the boys reached Corsicana just as the sun was rising in the east.

At that point, as they attempted to cross a small creek when something caught Jim's eye.

"Hold up," Jim whispered. "Let's see what this could be here in the stream."

After hiding themselves and their horses behind a thicket, they looked to see five Indians, mounted on beautiful steeds and equipped with single-shot Springfield rifles, riding down the middle of the stream. It appeared from a distance they were braves, most likely on their first raid. Among the group was an older brave with a feathered headdress, suggesting he was a chief of some sort. He carried a ceremonial spear with what appeared to be scalps hanging from one end.

The Indians moved stealthily and almost silently, apart from the noise their horses made jostling through the creek water beneath them.

As the braves grew closer, the boys carefully cocked their repeating rifles, held their breath, and said a silent prayer they would not be seen.

Suddenly, a mockingbird flew directly in front of Jim's horse, causing him to jump sideways. The braves were startled but recovered swiftly. In the blink of an eye, they raised their rifles to their shoulders. Bobby and Jim proved to be quicker, however, and managed to fire the first shots with their Remington Repeaters, causing death and confusion among the braves. The chief and the two braves that flanked him dropped immediately. The two in the back managed to fire a few shots before realizing they needed to turn quickly and escape. As they changed direction, Jim and Bobby continued to fire, killing both within fifty feet of the first volley.

Following the carnage, the scene before them was a terrible sight: five lives snuffed out with four appearing to be as young as themselves. They immediately knew they had to get as far away as soon as possible. The braves would no doubt be missed, and the boys were fearful the rest of their tribe would come looking for them soon. Bobby wanted to gather the lances of the fallen men, especially the chief's, but Jim warned they did not have time.

Instead, they spurred their horses and sprinted south through a line of trees for concealment. After a couple of miles, the pace was slowed to a lope, and then, after a couple more miles, to a trot. Finally, the horses and boys could catch their breath. They knew the horses had to be as fresh as possible in case they ran into the wandering tribe and had to escape quickly.

Though night had fallen, the moon was full, and they still hid beneath available cover when possible. They had no idea how many Indians were in the tribe or where they were.

When they reached the edge of what they believed to be Dallas county, they turned south, staying that course until morning. If they were right, they would end up somewhere around the settlement of Ennis. Several house fires were seen in the distance, but the boys did not check them out. They felt it was a safe assumption the Indians were wreaking havoc in the distance. They knew their lack of manpower could not effectively help against what was surely a tribe of many men.

The sun was rising in the east when they decided to stop. As best as they could figure, they were between the settlements of Corsicana and Ennis. If this was the case, home was so close they could taste it.

They found a clump of trees to bed down and hobbled their horses nearby. They slept deeply until about 4:00 in the afternoon when Bobby nudged Jim.

"Let's chance it and start early," Bobby said excitedly.

"No, not this close to home," Jim replied. "I would hate to get scalped when all we have to do is wait another three or four hours."

"You're right," Bobby conceded. "I'm just anxious."

For the rest of the evening, the boys sat in the thicket and talked about home, ever mindful of the possible danger that still surrounded them.

It was cold when evening came as it was January and darkness fell between 7:00 and 7:30. It was at this time they unhobbled their horses, mounted them, and began to head southwest. At this point, they guessed they were only about fifty miles from Spillar Ranch. They figured they would arrive at about 3:00 or 4:00 the following morning, if nothing prevented them from continuing forward.

The nearness of their destination inspired a shared exhilaration within the boys is difficult to express in plain words. It had been almost two years since they had been home.

Though Bobby was from West Columbia, a substantial distance from Mexia, he was considering taking on his old job at Spillar Ranch. Jim was confident the ranch would need the help as many of the workers left to fight in the Confederate army.

As they got closer to their destination, the boys said nothing, overwhelmed by the thoughts of what arriving at home would feel like. Though they couldn't know exactly what lay in front of them, they were both sure it was going to be a happy reunion and huge relief. All the trials they had faced in the two years they were gone would at last be worth it.

13

COMING HOME

At about 2:30 a.m., they came within view of the small settlement of Tehuacana sitting on the high hill. They swung west to avoid attracting attention and rode toward Mexia. Their excitement continued to grow.

When they finally reached Mexia, they rode directly down the middle of Main Street. As they crossed into the corporate limits of the town, a posse of gun-toting men surrounded them. The head of the group was Tom from the Spillar Ranch. He did not recognize Jim, but Jim recognized him.

"Tom," he said, "It's me, Jim!"

Upon recognition of his old friend, a big smile swept across Tom's face.

"Bring me that torch," Jim called out to a man on the edge of the group. "What are you doing back home? I thought you were fighting in the war against the Northern aggression."

"I was captured at Arkansas Post and escaped a few days ago with my friend, Bobby," Jim explained. "You remember Robert Johnson, don't you? He was working at the ranch and we joined the cause together."

"What are you doing here so early in the morning?" Tom asked. "A big group of Indians are on the prowl in these parts. By best estimate, over a thousand braves left the reservation at Fort Sill about a week ago. The leader of the group is called Chief Santana. He lost his son on a raid and is out to settle some scores. They say he carries his son's bones in a sack on his horse at all times."

"We noticed many houses burning from a distance between Ennis and Tehuacana," Bobby told Tom.

"Those houses were vacant, most likely," Tom replied. "Most farmers and ranchers had advanced warning and evacuated to nearby communities where they forted up."

The boys nodded, listening close to the information Tom offered.

"These Indians aren't stupid," Tom continued. "They usually don't attack unless the odds are in their favor."

Though the tribe had been estimated at about a thousand braves, the Indians were known to split up into smaller parties with most groups numbering less than a hundred warriors. Though substantially smaller, a group that size would still be difficult for the men to stave off. The typical small settlements were hardly more than that number but most of these men were hearty individuals who could shoot straight and ride hard. On the other hand, they were still faced a disadvantage as the braves spent their days learning to hunt and becoming warriors.

"We warned all the settlers in the vicinity of Mexia to come in for protection and defend the town," Tom said, looking the boys squarely in the eye. "As far as we know, everyone has answered the call."

"How long has this been going on – the fortification of the towns?"

"This is the third night and so far, it has been an effective strategy," Tom answered. "No one has been lost or harmed in any way. We were just lucky we were warned in time to protect ourselves."

"They weren't so luck in the western settlements like Jacksboro, Palo Pinto, and Weatherford," another man in the group said. "They were hit pretty hard."

Of course, those were the areas where the Indians first came into contact while on their murderous raids.

Though the military garrisons had been reinforced with militia at Fort Richardson in Jacksboro and Fort Belknap in Graham, the real soldiers had left to fight in the Civil War. That is not to say there weren't some excellent troopers, including Texas Rangers, within the group. Among these men were Charles Goodnight and Oliver Loving who were at the forefront of any fight. These men, along with civilians and the Texas militia, hunkered down at Fort Belknap.

During this time, Goodnight and Loving were looked upon as heroes by those who knew them and others who had only heard of them. Oliver Loving was an older man who took charge of the logistics of running a military camp. Goodnight's story was almost mythical in that he was a Texas Ranger, top hand as a cowboy, and excellent Indian battle strategist on the frontier. It is said that when he was only nine he rode with his parents all the way from Texas to Illinois on bareback. Both Loving and Goodnight were known as trailblazers, too, and had driven large cattle herds from Texas to New Mexico, Colorado, and Montana.

There were times, though, when the men had to take time off to protect their property and their lives. When the soldiers left to fight with the Confederacy, Goodnight and Loving were forced to form militia units just to survive.

Goodnight had a ranch that was one of the first to be attacked and no one presently had any idea what condition it was in. The Indians started their convergence at Elm Creek and the Brazos River in Young County. They followed it down into the middle of the state killing men, women, and children who lived on the farms and ranches. Goodnight's ranch was located on Elm Creek where the braves started their murderous rampage. The invasion, despite spreading throughout north central and parts of east Texas, would hence be known as the Elm Creek Raid.

The band of savages split up east of Weatherford, a small settlement east of Fort Worth. One group headed up through Denton County and then into east Texas while another group went south of Fort Worth into the Ennis and Fairfield areas of Central Texas. With no organized military contingent, the only choice for Texans was to gather together for protection.

"What is the state of affairs out at the Spillar Ranch?" Jim asked Tom.

"They've got about forty men boarded up in the bunkhouse and the main house," Tom answered. "The horses are in the corrals and protected. As you know, the horses are the first things the Indians will try to take."

"What about Charlie," Jim asked with a bit of trepidation. "Is she alright?"

"She's fine," Tom reassuringly replied. "I'm not sure she ever got over you leaving, though."

"Is it possible to get to the ranch tonight?" Jim asked.

"I think it would be best to wait until the sun is high in the sky," Tom warned. "The men are a little skittish and trigger happy due to the lack of sleep they've had in the past few days. These men have had some really ghastly experiences during this period of time."

Jim told Tom and the rest of the group about their experience with the four braves and the chief. As he told the story, he and Bobby both became a little sad, but they knew they had no choice but to kill the Indians.

"Don't be hard on yourselves," Tom told them. "You had no choice. It was kill or be killed."

"I'm not sure what will happen if the siege doesn't end within the week," Tom continued. "The men at Spillar are running low on food, but they have a sufficient amount of ammunition. They are getting edgy and concerned about their families."

"What are the alternatives?" Bobby asked.

"Not many are open to us," Tom replied. "If they don't get help within a few days, they will run out of food. Their rations have been short since they arrived here. They need help in the way of a large military unit. Nothing less will force the Indians back over the Red River and into their territory again."

"Most of the Mexia citizens and people in the surrounding areas have barricaded themselves in the town center waiting for the main attack," Tom continued. "So far, they've only been subject to small attacks to gauge their own strength. They've killed three Indians and wounded several more, but the injured Indians were able to remain on their horses and get away."

One of the men in the group, who had arrived at about midnight, stepped forward and General Sterling Price and his regiment was just over the Louisiana border. What's more, The General didn't seem to recognize the gravity of the situation. The man suggested that if someone could ride to his headquarters and make him aware of the danger, he could kill or run what was left of the savages back to the territories.

Tom, whose leadership everyone trusted, said they could send someone on a fast horse to see if they could speak to the General and ask him to come and help them evade danger.

"I'll go!" Jim offered, speaking up quickly.

"It would be more practical to send two riders for a better chance of getting through," Bobby added.

"That's a good idea," Tom said. "Each man should take two extra horses. One horse can be ridden down relatively quickly in a pursuit. It's important that someone gets through and bring us help."

"Tom, can I bring Charlie?" Jim asked. "She has always been durable, smart, and fast."

"That's a fine idea," Tom replied. "She is in the corral near the big barn – the one with the tack room."

"Thanks, Tom," Jim said excitedly. "I appreciate it!"

At last Jim would reunite with his beautiful and trusted friend.

14

RIDING FOR THE CAVALRY

There about two hours of darkness left when Jim arrived at Spillar ranch. He had to be careful not to be shot by mistake by the people at the ranch. He stopped abruptly about a hundred feet out and hollered that he was coming in. A voice from the barn told him to come in, but to keep his hands away from his guns. After he got closer inside the ranch, Jim was recognized, resulting in a happy reunion. He explained he was there to pick up Charlie so he could ride her to get help from General Sterling Price. With that news, the men got to work finding Jim a lariat, saddle, and bridle. One of the ranch hands went to fetch Charlie and brought her to Jim.

At the site of her old friend, Charlie was raring, nickering, and joyously nodding her head. Jim was just as happy to see her and, once in the saddle, rode from the ranch as quickly as possible, knowing he had to get far away from the Indian's center of concentration. He rode forth with the idea that he would ride one horse and before he got weary, he would change his saddle to the other horse to keep the horses fresh as possible. Initially, Jim planned to bring two extra horses, but once he knew Charlie would take the trip with him, he felt comfortable bringing only one extra steed with him. Charlie was so strong and steady; he had no doubts she would handle the journey well.

Once away from the ranch, Jim headed east, carefully skirting the settlement of Teague and then between the small towns of Fairfield and Buffalo. He knew the Indians were likely circling the communities, waiting for an opportunity to strike. The live oak thickets could hide plenty of braves, not to be seen until it was too late.

Though the path was dangerous, Jim had no choice but to ride on. Even Charlie seemed to sense the danger. He rode hard all night until the sun began to rise in the east.

Sensing that Charlie was growing weary, Jim leaned forward and rubbed her neck gently, reminding her of his fondness for his old friend. He then guided the horses into a thicket of live oaks and changed his saddle from Charlie to his other mount. The new horse kept a good pace helped him move farther from the more dangerous areas. During his ride, Jim had close calls with some Indians, but they were in small groups and unwilling to commit without a larger group behind them.

Due to the desperate state the people of the Indian-ravaged areas were in, Jim decided to continue after the sun was high in the sky. He continued riding all day without stopping for a noon meal. Instead, he had a bit of jerky Tom had given him to eat. From time to time, he would reach into his vest pocket and take a bite, staving off hunger for a while longer. The only time he would stop was to rest the horses and change his mount. Keeping the horses fresh was crucial in enemy territory.

At about 3:00 in the afternoon, Jim spotted some outriders far in the distance. While they didn't appear to be Indians, he wasn't close enough to tell for sure. They seemed to be riding straight for him, so he pulled behind some bushes to identify them before he was seen. As they got closer, Jim could see that the front rider had a small flag known was the Stars and Bars, the official flag of the Confederacy.

Jim put the reins in his teeth and rode out with his hands pointed to the sky. He knew to be careful because there were dangerous people in the area. A lot of the military were known to shoot first and ask questions later.

Upon spotting Jim, the troopers pulled their horses' reins and slowed to a stop.

"We're from General Sterling Price's regiment," they said, looking Jim up and down.

Jim identified himself and told them of his mission to find the military to help the beleaguered citizens of north and central Texas.

"I'm Lieutenant Leroy Vann," one of the men said. "The regiment is about ten miles behind us. General Price has outriders to the northwest, west, and southwest. We are aware that people fleeing the danger is a problem, but the numbers and locations of the Indians are yet to be determined."

"Lieutenant Vann," Jim began, "The braves number about a thousand. They are split up, but each group is sizeable and cannot be met on a battlefield with our scattered groups.

We don't have the ammunition or manpower to defeat them. What's more, we're running really low on food."

"It'll take us about three hours to get a battalion up. It is made up of about five hundred riders with the rest following in about half a day. It takes time to move large bodies of men."

After gathering the battalion, the march back to Mexia would take about fifteen hours. With that time frame, they could expect to arrive at around eight the next morning. No matter the amount of time it took them, they knew they would be greeted by a group of appreciative citizens.

Lieutenant Vann motioned to his two scouts, bringing them to the front of the small group.

"Ride back to the main body of soldiers and convey to the General that the Indians have been found. Tell him to bring the troops, post haste."

"I'm sending both of you to improve the chance of the message getting through," He continued. "This is extremely important. The lives of countless men, women, and children hang in the balance. We will wait here for you to return and then have Mr. Walker guide us to the besieged areas."

With that, the scouts saluted, spurred their mounts, and rode east as quickly as their horses could carry them.

During the next three hours, Jim spent some time describing the hostile areas they would encounter on their journey.

"It has been about two years since I've been a resident of the territory," Jim explained. "I was away fighting for the Confederacy and have since escaped imprisonment from the Northern soldiers. Tom Green is the ranch foreman and sometimes Texas Ranger. He will be able to help us with the most critical information about the area."

"Do you think General Price will be open to others' opinions?" Jim asked, turning toward Lieutenant Vann.

"Unlike most Field Grade Officers, General Price encourages input from other sources and considers it carefully when making his final decisions," Vann assured Jim.

When the conversation of the future battle dwindled, the men began to speak more personally.

As they spoke, Jim learned that Lieutenant Vann had graduated from the University of Mississippi at Oxford with a major in architecture.

"I wanted to build big, wonderful things like bridges and buildings and here I am, destroying those very things," Leroy said sadly. "These creations are more than just things. They are the idea of bringing something of substance into existence. I know I sound like a nut, but I really believe I can create something useful for mankind before I'm gone."

"You don't sound like a nut," Jim said, looking up into the sky. "I think everyone should feel like you do."

With those few sentences, Jim knew that Leroy was different than others he had known in the past.

"Do you have family in the area?" Leroy asked.

"I'm not married, and my folks are in Jackson, Mississippi. I haven't seen 'em in almost four years. How about you? Do you have family?"

"I do," Leroy answered thoughtfully. "I have a wife, a girl I married when I graduated from college, and we have a son who is almost a year old. I haven't seen my wife in over a year and I've never seen my son."

A faint noise rose in the distance and Leroy quickly jumped to his feet.

"I think I hear the battalion coming," He said, motioning to Jim.

The two stood side by side, squinting to see if it was really the soldiers coming into view. Sure enough, the large cavalry could soon be distinguished, even in the early twilight, by their flags and military uniforms.

Leroy turned to Jim and put one hand on his shoulder.

"I guess we'd better go back to the military politeness of you addressing me by my military rank, but I'll always be Leroy to you," Lieutenant Vann said, shaking Jim's hand.

As the troopers got closer, Jim could not help but notice the man leading them with a large plume in his hat and the stars of a general on his uniform. He was sure he had finally spotted General Sterling in the flesh.

It was not long before the battalion was before them and General Sterling was asking Lieutenant Vann to bring him up to date.

"General Sterling," Vann replied, "This is Jim Walker. He can be more helpful in describing the train, estimating distances, and gauging the number of hostiles. He worked on a ranch at Mexia before leaving for active duty at Arkansas Post. He was captured and escaped and has only been back in the area for a few days."

"Very good," General Sterling replied, nodding at Jim.

"The area consists of small hills, sir," Jim began. "There is also blue stem and prairie grass. Most of the trees are post oak thickets. This is mostly what we will encounter between here and Mexia."

"What do you estimate would be the best way to navigate that terrain with the danger we'll be facing?" General Sterling asked Jim with pointed focus.

Jim, a bit nervous about offering advice to such an important man, took a deep breath.

"I would put some outriders a couple miles in front to ride as fast as they can to get to Mexia. They can warn us of any danger ahead and alert the townspeople to our arrival," Jim began, becoming more confident as he spoke. "As far as numbers, I only know for certain there are a lot. I've heard as high as over a thousand, but I think that's more than reality. My guess is between five and six hundred. Only the Indians themselves know for sure."

"And what about the tribes involved?" Sterling asked, listening carefully to Jim's well-considered words.

"The tribes we have encountered are mostly Comanches with some Kiowas. In my experience, I've determined the Comanches are the best light cavalry in the world. They must not be taken lightly. I've had some experience as a Texas Ranger, and I know the Rangers consider the Comanche a force to be reckoned with. Your helping us means a lot, sir," Jim added. "The souls you've agreed to protect need you desperately."

With that, General Price told Lieutenant Vann to take his unit and ride ahead of the battalion in case anything of concern was discovered.

Lt. Vann suggested that Jim join him and General Price agreed.

After riding ahead and turning their well-rested horses west and commenced to a trot. Just as Jim had on his way to meet the battalion, the men decided to stop every couple of hours to allow the horses to rest and the larger unit to catch up from behind. They also left colorful pieces of cloth on the trail the General's scouts could follow.

On their trek, Jim noticed numerous fires which seemed to more burning ranches and farms. The Indians had clearly been busy overnight. Bowing his head slightly, Jim silently prayed that the families made it out safely. When midnight came, the moon escaped the clouds and shone brightly, lighting the path before them. This was helpful as it improved their visibility, but dangerous as it improved the enemies' visibility, too.

After about five uneventful hours of riding closer and closer to their destination, they encountered a saddleback mountain and saw twenty or so braves mounted on horseback, looking down into the valley.

Jim and the troopers quietly slowed to a stop. They had been riding inside a line of trees making them difficult to see, knowing full well they could come across a group of savage braves at any moment.

From their stance, Jim could see they were outnumbered but he didn't think they were outgunned. The men amongst him were equipped with repeating rifles, while the Indians most likely had the old single-shot, breech-loading rifles. Jim knew such old weapons couldn't fire as much in a short amount of time as the repeating rifles his group carried.

"Let's take them," Lt. Vann said, saying the same words Jim was thinking. "We can ride around behind them and attack. We know where they are, but they don't know where we are. That's a necessary advantage."

Jim and Lt. Vann's group moved through the line of trees past the group of Indians as quietly as they could. After reaching a spot they deemed safe, they tied their horses to some trees and climbed the back of the hill on foot, careful not to step on any dry limbs or twigs.

After gaining a position from behind, Jim and Lt. Vann silently counted the number of braves whose bodies were highlighted by the full moon. There were eighteen Indians, all on horseback. After assessing the fight that lay before them, Lt. Vann assigned each of the troopers particular targets. This would ensure that several of the men would not fire in the same direction, allowing others to escape and creating chaos.

Most of the troopers were given responsibility for at least two Indians. Then, Lt. Vann, explained that they were to begin firing when he dropped his arm. When the order was given, the soldiers began firing and the Indians dropped from their horses with no discernable noise but for the deafening fire from the rifles. When the firing stopped, there was no sound or movement from the braves in the distance.

When they were certain they were in no more danger, they mounted their horses and rode toward their destination.

When they were about twelve miles southeast of Mexia, they stopped at a small settlement called Teague. At first, the people of Teague were wary of the strangers. Once Jim and Lt. Vann had identified themselves and explained their mission, they were welcomed as friends.

"I think we should stop here and ride in with General Price and his army," Jim told Lt. Vann. "We should act as a buffer before the whole force descends on Mexia."

"The troops should be getting here before long," said Lt. Vann. "We lost some time when we stopped to take care of the Indians back there."

Jim felt it was good policy to let the people of Teague know that a large body of troopers would be arriving soon. With the darkness looming, a large herd of horses could cause the townspeople think imminent danger was heading their way. Such confusion could cause a very dangerous situation.

15

THE CAVALRY ARRIVES IN MEXIA

When Jim went to warn the citizens of Teague about the battalion's arrival, he found a Texas Ranger oversaw the settlement. The Ranger was kind and offered Jim and the rest of the troopers fresh coffee, which was greatly appreciated. They were on their second cup when they heard the thunderous rumble of horses' hooves striking the soft sod surrounding the settlement.

It was the Calvary arriving with all their force, riding in from the open prairie to the east. General Sterling Price rode grandly into view, heroically leading his men to rescue the area of the dangers that threatened.

Upon spotting the general, Jim and Lt. Vann mounted their horses and rode out to meet him.

"This is hostile territory," Lt. Vann told General Price. "But, heck, everything in these parts is probably occupied by Indians now."

"I don't want to speak out of turn by telling the general how to run his military affairs," Jim added hesitantly. "But I think it would be practical to leave a detachment here in case the Indians should attack this settlement in the meantime. The rest of the battalion could go on to Mexia and wherever they are needed. I'm of the opinion that once the Indians see the Cavalry in full force, they will head back to their own territory."

"You are right, Jim," General Price agreed. "The Cavalry needs to relieve the citizens of Mexia and the surrounding areas."

Then, after locking eyes with Jim, he added, "I appreciate a local such as yourself sharing your knowledge with me. Your suggestion is sound."

In a short time, it was decided that the general would leave with a detachment from Teague. With a forward wave of his hand, he led the troops out northwest toward Mexia. As they left, the townspeople gathered to cheer the men on, a combined effort to show their thanks.

Even though Jim was dead tired, the gratitude displayed filled him with renewed vigor. Riding astride Charlie, he couldn't help but feel a little bit of pride.

As they rode to Mexia, numerous Indians were spotted but they kept their distance and no unfriendly initiatives were made. Finally, the forces arrived in Mexia to the stressed cheers of its citizens.

Jim immediately spotted Tom, who ran out of the crowd.

"They really are glad you're here," Tom said breathlessly. "They were attacked last night and lost three men. If the Indians had sustained the assault, the men here would have run out of ammunition. It would have turned to hand-to-hand with rifle barrels and hatchets. Thank God you're here!"

"Have you heard anything from Bobby?" Jim asked worriedly.

"No. Not a word," Tom replied, shaking his head sadly.

"I hope nothing has happened to him," Jim said. "I saw a lot of Indian activity as I rode east to get the army. Houses and ranches were burning to the ground."

"Hopefully Bobby is still riding north of where you encountered General Price and his army."

"I hope so," Jim replied dazedly.

About thirty minutes after the troops arrived, a train of supply wagons rolled in carrying ammunition and food. One wagon was left in Teague as all of the surrounding settlements were down to almost nothing.

With sentries posted, the soldiers and citizens settled down to enjoy a meal of army chow. Though it wasn't the best meal any of them had ever tasted, it seemed so at the time.

At noon, the soldiers were beyond exhausted and dragged about the town. It had been two days since they'd had a good night's sleep. The citizens suffered the same malady, not having eaten or slept in almost a week.

As Jim sacked out below one of the supply wagons, his head barely hit the dirt before he fell into a deep slumber. After sleeping for about four sound hours, he was jostled from his sleep by someone shaking him.

Through his bleary, sleep-filled eyes, he saw a figure standing over him. He recognized the figure almost immediately, but thought his eyes deceived him. Was he still asleep? Was he really seeing who he thought he saw?

"Bobby?" Jim said sleepily. "Could that really be you?"

"It's me, Jim," Bobby answered quietly. "I can't blame you for being surprised. I didn't think I was going to make it there for a while. Fortunately, that horse I picked at the Weatherbys could run fast as the dickens."

"What happened?" Jim asked.

"I came across a group of about ten Indians and they chased me for about five miles or so. It was my fault. I misjudged where they might be. My carelessness almost cost me my life."

The reality began to set in for Jim that his friend had made it out safe.

"I know one thing, Jim," Bobby added. "Those Indians are excellent horsemen and skilled warriors."

Jim nodded in agreement as he had witnessed the same thing. Then his attention turned to Bobby's condition.

"Are you hungry? Have you slept at all?" He asked, knowing that Bobby must have been famished and exhausted.

"Well, I'm starving," Bobby confessed, "but I don't know if I can keep my eyes open long enough to eat."

After the army cook rustled up something for Bobby, Jim took him over to the supply wagon. Bobby sat in the shade of an oak tree and began to eat. After taking only a few bites, he slumped over, fast asleep. Jim then stretched him out and placed a saddle blanket under his head. His friend had lived a tough couple of days and deserved his rest.

That evening, at about dark, a group up men rode up from the direction of Tehuacana and asked to see the man in charge.

"Well, I'm a Texas Ranger and have been the man responsible until General Price arrived today," Tom told them. "If I understand correctly, the civilian militia is my responsibility and the army is under General Price. The groups work together for the common good."

Listening from nearby, another man stepped forward.

"I'm Charles Goodnight and I'm in charge of new arrivals," Goodnight said. "I am here with my friend and business associate, Oliver Loving. We have been riding hard from the Jacksboro and Weatherford areas. There's a large war army out in that direction and we've been chasing them."

Tom was taken aback. He'd heard of Charles Goodnight, but never met him until now.

"The army has about five hundred surrounded in a box canyon about ten miles from here," Goodnight continued. "If they knew our numbers, they wouldn't stay surrounded for long. We know our small group wouldn't threaten them at all. Our troops have been alerted that General Price has arrived, and they desperately need his help to take care of the problem. If the battalion can get there soon, they might be able to secure their position before the Indians realize their weakness."

Jim ran back to the oak tree where his friend slept.

"Bobby, wake up! We're going to join forces with Charlie Goodnight and the Texas Rangers!" Jim shouted excitedly.

"You're kidding me, right?!" Bobby jumped straight to his feet.

"Just saddle your horse and hurry or we'll be left behind!" Jim replied.

After mounting their horses and heading out with the group, Bobby and Jim couldn't believe their luck to be part of such an important mission with such important men.

When they had ridden for about an hour, Goodnight rode up to the two boys and Tom, who was riding with them.

"You people know this country better than any of us," Goodnight said. "The Indians are only about two or three miles to the northwest. We need a good strategy or we'll get a lot of people killed. I think we need to make a wide sweep around the area to scout the area where the Indians are located."

Tom agreed and headed out with the boys to follow Goodnight's suggestion.

After arriving at their destination, the three men set about encircling the canyon. From their vantage point, they assessed the situation before riding back to share the word with the army that waited in Mexia. As they rode back, the men each silently wondered about the casualties that would be incurred during an assault on an entrenched enemy. It didn't matter, though. They knew they had to push forward and protect the citizens of surrounding areas.

Once back in town, the men rode toward the waiting army, anxious to tell them what they had seen.

General Price came forth to meet them.

"What's the situation?" He asked. "What do you think can be done to make this a fair fight?"

"General Price," Jim said, this time with more confidence, "as we circled their encampment, I noticed they had their horses at the northeast corner tied to rope lines. If we could go in and run off their horse herd, the Indian threat would be over. An Indian without a horse is an Indian that can't win."

General Price and the men agreed it was a good idea. Furthermore, it would likely keep the casualties to a minimum.

The men were saddled up and ready to go at 7:00 p.m. with the attack planned for only an hour after that. The strategy was for most of the battalion to feint an attack against the main group of Indians while approximately twelve men cut the rope lines of the Indians' horses and took them far enough away to where they could not be reached on foot.

To ensure the Indians did not become a dangerous light cavalry again, the horses would be slaughtered. No man liked the idea of doing such a thing, but knew it was a necessary measure to protect the frontier. Without their horses, the Indians wouldn't be able to stage another massive attack on the settlers for a long time. As it was Jim's idea, he and Bobby followed the men who went to fetch the horses.

As the battalion distracted the main group of Indians, a group of braves stood guarding the horses, so a few of the men in Jim and Bobby's group snuck up behind them and killed them dead. At the same time, the other men cut the rope lines and herded the horses away from the Indian camp. In just a few minutes, it was over.

That was easy, Jim thought. *Too easy.*

But, he thought, the number of men in the battalion is what made the operation so seamless. That, of course, and, though he was too humble to say so, his idea of removing the horses from the Indians' grasp. Knowing they wouldn't have such an easy time of traveling the area made Jim breathe a sigh of relief. There had been too many families killed, too many women raped, and too many buildings burned to the ground. The people of the settlements deserved to have their lives back, and Jim aimed to do everything he could to help make that happen.

The next morning, Charlie Goodnight talked to General Price about taking a Comanche translator down to speak with the Indians. Price agreed and sent them on their way.

Once in the presence of the Indian settlement, Charlie held up a white bedsheet to signal his wish to parley with the Indians. The old chief, who had directed his men to commit the devastating raids, walked out to meet Charlie.

Jim, who had secretly tagged along, watched as the chief threw his hands up in the air and spoke loudly, though his words were indiscernible with the translator's interpretation out of earshot. When the chief was finished, Charlie turned to walk away, but the chief motioned him back. Jim later learned that the chief refused to yield, and Charlie told him to go to hell. If the chief wasn't willing to compromise, then Charlie threatened to kill all his horses and his braves.

"That's what I'd really like to do," Charlie had said.

That is when he had turned to walk off, but the old chief called out to him and said he would agree to Charlie's terms.

As a result, early the next morning a mounted guard surrounded the Indians while they surrendered their weapons. As was expected, a few young braves tried to escape with their weapons, but most didn't make it. Only a few managed to scurry away and disappear out of sight before the guards could catch them.

Though it wasn't known at the time, the escapees would eventually steal horses from the ranches and farms in the area and take up residence in the houses that had been abandoned there.

After all the weapons had been surrendered, Charlie told the chief to take his men home. Upon Charlie's request, a small group of men from the battalion followed the braves until they reached their sanctuary across the Red River at Fort Sill. The old chief was angry, but grateful that most of his men had been spared.

At 10:00 a.m., the chief had his men in a formation of columns, ready to start their long march back home. The chief asked if he could have some horses to help with the trek, but General Price and Charlie were unwavering in their decision about not allowing the tribe to have any horses. If they had, Charlie felt sure they would be raiding and killing again before they got to Hillsboro.

As the Indians made their way back to their territory, followed by one hundred soldiers with repeating rifles, a few men stayed back and took on the grizzly chore of killing the horses. Though some horses were spared and given to men for their efforts in battle, the rest of them were bound to die. Slaughtering the horses was something no man wanted to do and a very unpleasant task.

16

LIFE GETTING BACK TO NORMAL

Most of the farmers and ranchers in the Mexia region had adequate warning to seek safety in the town. The buildings that burned during the previous nights had been vacant with their residents long gone to hunker down with the townspeople. Their fate was substantially better than the people of Palo Pinto and Jack County on the northwestern frontier. Unfortunately for the people there, they were the first to encounter the hostile Indians and had no advance warning. They were not able to summon a battalion or loose the braves' horses like the men in Mexia had. Despite their initial poor fortune, they were fortunate to benefit from the heroic actions of the men with whom Jim had fought beside, from those in the civilian militia to the professional soldiers under the guidance of General Sterling Price.

When the men of the town were certain they had successfully removed the threat of future raids, individuals began to prepare for the next move. After returning to Mexia, Charlie Goodnight and Oliver Loving gathered their horses and commenced to say goodbye to the townspeople.

After seeing them off, Bobby and Jim finally stopped to realize how tired they were. Sneaking off with a bedroll, they found somewhere to sleep for about twelve hours. When they woke, they went directly to Spillar Ranch and renewed friendships with people they had not seen in over two years.

After arriving at the ranch, the first-person Jim recognized was Mrs. Spillar who stood on the front porch of the main house. When she saw the boys, she went running toward them. Upon reaching them, she threw her arms around first one and then the other. She was crying and shouting joyously at the same time.

The feeling of her arms wrapped around them was like a mother's embrace. It was so good to be back.

Standing back to look at the boys, Mrs. Spillars eyes filled with happy tears. She couldn't believe they were standing right in front of her once more.

"Mr. Spillar went out on the range to check on the livestock once General Price and the army arrived in town," she told them.

"There's a good chance the cows are alright," Jim said assuredly. "The Indians don't much like cows since they only eat the grass they feed their buffalos."

Jim didn't tell her that the Indians would sometimes kill cows as an act of vengeance. This kind of attack was characteristic of a killing raid, but not one meant to just steal horses.

As they caught up on the time gone by, five riders were seen coming across the prairie to the southwest.

"There's Mr. Spillar now!" Mrs. Spiller exclaimed, leaping to her feet.

The men rode up into the yard where she and the boys were standing. Mr. Spillar did not know that Jim and Bobby had returned, since he had been out of Mexia for three days. When Jim picked up Charlie at the ranch, it was dark and only a couple of ranch hands were aware of his presence.

While the raids were happening, Mr. Spillar had fortified the ranch into a strongpoint and stayed there to act as commander in charge. Since learning that the threat was over, he had felt safe enough to go and check on his cattle.

As expected, Mr. Spillar was thrilled to see Jim and Bobby back on the ranch.

"How were you boys able to return while your military unit is still in the field?" He asked.

"The 10th Texas is no more," Jim said sadly. "All of the men were either killed or captured at Arkansas Post."

"As for us, we were captured and held on a boat that was sailing north on the Mississippi to a prison camp," Bobby added. "We escaped by jumping overboard and managed to get away by hiding behind some timber. We think we were headed to Camp Douglas in Illinois."

"How were the cattle," Jim asked, wondering about Mr. Spillar's findings on the prairie. "Did the Indians kill a substantial amount of your herd?"

"No," Mr. Spillar answered. "We were really lucky the military arrived in time. They must have thought they had time to kill the livestock later."

"You owe a debt of gratitude to the military, Mr. Spillar," Bobby said proudly. "And Jim, too. He rode almost to the

Louisiana border to find General Price and bring his forces back to Mexia."

"Bobby is being modest, Mr. Spillar," Jim rushed to add. "He took a different route for the same purpose. It is only by matter of chance that I encountered the general first."

Both Mr. and Mrs. Spillar were overwhelmed knowing the lengths the boys had gone to in hopes of saving the town. Two young men they had not seen in two years were suddenly back and had risked their lives to save not only their community, but the whole area from Fort Belknap in the northwest to the pine forests of east Texas.

"I believe a celebration is in order to honor your bravery," Mr. Spillar said, beaming with pride. "We'll invite everyone in the area to show their appreciation for what you both have done."

The boys felt a bit taken aback by the idea of a gathering to honor themselves, but they were happy to take the opportunity to see old friends and make new acquaintances.

"We might even meet some girls," Bobby said with a wink. "Our love life has certainly suffered the past two years."

"What's a love life?" Jim replied, chuckling a bit.

Laughing for the first time in a long time, the boys finally began to relax after feeling nothing but stress and heartache over the past couple of years. No matter who they met at the party, they knew a good time would be had by all.

17

THE CELEBRATION

That evening, the boys were invited to dinner in the main house and everyone was in good spirits. After eating a good, hearty meal, the boys headed out to the bunkhouse to enjoy a sound sleep. They were surprised to find their bunks exactly as they had left them two years earlier. Laying their heads on familiar pillows, they had the best night's sleep they'd had since the last night before they left the ranch.

The next morning, they got up, ate breakfast, and saddled their riding horses. Once atop their mounts, they went to work on the ranch as though they had never left.

Jim could not believe the joy of being back in the saddle, herding cattle, and doing the things he used to consider as mundane ranch chores. Just having enough food to eat, a comfortable bed, and not being in constant danger was almost overwhelming for the first few days. Though working at the ranch again was like a dream come true, the boys weren't sure what lay ahead in their future. The war was still raging between the Union and the South.

"If they form a new unit, we can join and go back and serve in the war, but I'm going to work here on the ranch until that day occurs," Jim told Bobby.

"That sounds good to me," Bobby replied.

The gathering to honor Jim and Bobby was also going to celebrate the end of the Indian threat. It was to be held on a Saturday night in the new Mexia community center. This would be the first event in the facility and would effectively christen the new building. Jim and Bobby were excited. They had never been the guests of honor at anything before.

The week passed quickly and Saturday night and the celebration were upon them. Bobby and Jim had nothing to wear except their old Confederate uniforms, which were in shreds. Before the celebration, the city of Mexia, led by Mrs. Spillar bought an assortment of clothes for each boy. They each received two pairs of khakis and one pair of heavy work trousers, three work shirts and one dress shirt, and a pair of work and dress boots each. They also got to pick out underwear, handkerchiefs, and a hat of their choosing.

When the boys took their baths in the horse tank and got dressed up, they both felt very special. Neither boy ever had this much wardrobe in their whole lives and knew who to thank for their good fortune: the Spillars and the good people of Mexia. They mounted their horses and rode from the ranch to the convention center, feeling very humble but blessed.

Jim was a ruggedly handsome young man, standing six feet tall. His jet-black hair and deep blue eyes, combined with his confident manner, were only a few of the qualities that made him so attractive. Bobby, fairly slight of build, had short blond hair, hazel eyes, and a sweet temperament that everyone loved.

When they arrived, the convention center was already crowded. A small band in the corner was playing a familiar song called "Dixie". A tear came to Jim' eye when he thought of his old military buddies who were most likely still in the prison camp at Camp Douglas in Chicago. The boys felt so blessed to have survived the battle at Arkansas Post, the encounter at the Weatherby's farm, and the Indian raids in Texas. They had weathered all the excitement they could for a while.

It wasn't long after they arrived that they spotted Mr. and Mrs. Spillar, who motioned for them to join them where they were standing. It wasn't long before they commenced to introducing them to all the people who had gathered to honor them in the hall. Though they met many people that evening, there was one person who stood out among the rest. She was a little blonde with blue eyes and Jim thought she was just beautiful.

"Who is she?" Jim asked Mrs. Spillar. "Does she live in Mexia?"

"Jim!" Answered Mrs. Spillar. "Surely you remember her! That's Laura Pruitt!"

"Not the skinny, little freckle-faced girl who was about four feet high when I left for the army?" Jim asked in disbelief.

"That's her!" Mrs. Spillar answered. "She's grown up quite a lot since you've seen her last."

"Yes, she has." Jim replied.

Jim couldn't believe his yes. Laura was not only beautiful but had a sense of culture about her. Still reeling, he pulled Bobby aside.

"I think I'm in love," Jim told him.

"You'd better get to know her before you ask her to marry you!" Bobby laughed.

"Aw, she would never look twice at me," Jim said sheepishly. "She could have her pick of any man she wanted."

By this time, the convention center was full. People had come from as far as Groesbeck and Fairfield. The party was a grand affair. The band consisted of a guitar, fiddle, piano, and a bearded fellow blowing harmoniously into a jug. The dances varied from slow two steps and waltzes to fast polkas and the popular square-dance.

About halfway through the celebration, Mr. Spillar made his way to a makeshift stage and loudly announced he would like to speak.

The crowd hushed and turned their attention to him.

"First, I'd like to honor the memories of those who have fallen in defense of the town. I think it would be appropriate to have a granite monument erected in their names. My family will happily purchase the stones and it is my hope that the inscriptions will be paid for by citizen contributions."

The crowd murmured excitedly. Everyone thought it was an excellent idea to commemorate those who had been lost in the effort to protect their lives. A man took the initiative to grab a wastebasket and began to pass it to gather contributions.

"I'd also like to thank all of you citizens for your unselfish acts and courage during this dangerous time," Mr. Spillar began. Most of all, I'd like to thank two young men whose heroic actions helped save this town. Some of you will recognize these fellows as former ranch hands on my ranch. After that, they entered the service and eventually escaped capture to fight many battles and finally bring General Sterling Price and his men to stop the hostile Indians who threatened our lives and communities. Come up here and let the citizens know who you are."

As Jim and Bobby made their way to the front, Mr. Spillar continued to relate the details of their stories, including their experiences at Arkansas Post and the Weatherby farm.

"Please, everyone, come forward and shake their hands!" Mr. Spillar said, stepping back to allow the crowd to thank Jim and Bobby themselves.

Of all the people who came forward, the boys noticed there were several young ladies who were not bashful in expressing their gratitude.

And to think, Jim mused, *all of this happened because his horse could jump higher than his father's back in Mississippi.*

Life was an amazing adventure and Jim and Bobby were living it to its fullest.

18

JIM MEETS WIFE

At the celebration, Jim did get a dance with Laurie Pruitt. As a matter of fact, she asked him for a dance. He was surprised at the invitation and readily admitted he was not a good dancer.

"That's alright," Laurie told him with a twinkle in her eye. "I'm not a good Indian fighter, but I can teach you to dance. I'll leave the Indian fight up to you, if that's alright."

The night passed swiftly and Jim asked Laurie if he could see her home. She happily agreed and Jim could not believe his good fortune to accompany such a beautiful girl. He was quite inexperienced with the ladies or any ladies. Though he was excited to take her home, he was especially nervous about one thing: he had no way to get home except his horse. Mrs. Spillar, who overheard Jim's invitation to Laurie, leaned forward and whispered in his ear.

"If you need a buggy to take her home, we've brought an extra. We can tie Charlie on our buggy to get back to the ranch."

Jim was overwhelmed and it showed on his face. He looked into Laurie's eyes and knew, after only a short period of time, she was the one.

Before leaving, Jim knew the proper thing to do was to ask Laurie's parents for permission to accompany her home. Her parents agreed with their blessing and Jim and Laurie set out to her family's property.

On the way, they stopped by a running creek with a gurgling spring. It was nice and peaceful, sitting in the buggy watching the water trickle over the rocks in the stream. As they sat there, Jim couldn't help but be nervous. Actually, he couldn't help but be scared to death. He had never been alone with a female except his sister and his mother. He was unsure of what to do or say.

Laurie came to the rescue when she asked him if he had a girl when he left for the army. Jim decided to be completely honest and told her she was the first girl he had been alone with in his whole life. She reached over and squeezed his hand.

"Well, you're the first boy I've ever been on a sort-of date with, too. I've never been alone with a boy either."

Knowing that, Jim relaxed a bit. They sat and talked for almost an hour and time flew by. It seemed they could keep talking forever.

"I love talking with you," Laurie told him, "but my family will be worried if I don't get home soon."

She reached over and squeezed Jim's hand. Completely smitten, he leaned in to kiss her on the cheek when she suddenly turned her head and their lips met. He was so excited he almost couldn't stand it.

After holding their lips together for a moment, they both leaned back.

"Is that the way it's done?" Jim asked, trying to keep his composure.

"I don't know, but it was wonderful!" Laurie replied with a wide smile on her face.

With that, Jim set about taking Laurie home. As the horses' hooves treaded through the creek water on the way, the two excitedly planned for a real date. Both knew their future was uncertain as Jim would likely have to return to active military service soon.

As they rode, Jim thought about Laurie. Though he had no commitment from her, he knew she was the one. At the same time, Laurie was thinking the same about him. He knew he couldn't ask her for a commitment until he had some certainty in his life. By the time they arrived at her house, Jim knew what he wanted to do, but so much depended on the war.

As the buggy pulled up to Laurie's house, they couldn't help but talk about what they future might hold.

"Can I see you again?" Jim asked sheepishly. "Would Saturday night be OK?"

"Of course, it's fine with me," Laurie blushed." But you'll have to get permission from my parents."

She squeezed his hand just as she had done at the creek.

"I really would love to go on a full date with you." She told him shyly.

It would be her first date with a boy, and she was glad it was him. Before climbing down from the buggy, she softly reached around his neck and pulled him close to give him a real kiss.

"I'll see you next Saturday night," she said, pulling away. "If I can't go, I'll get word to you somehow."

Smiling, Jim watched Laurie as she made it safely into her home. He drove home on a cloud. He didn't know much about love, but an overwhelming feeling had captured him. As he came to the gates of the ranch, he was sure he had never seen the sky so blue or the stars so bright.

All was right with the world.

Upon his return, he unhitched the team of horses and gave each horse some oats to eat and fresh water to drink.

Charlie had been in the corral and ran to Jim when she saw him ride up. He knew he hadn't spent enough time with his old friend but promised he would from now on. He felt first-rate about his good fortune and how God had smiled down upon him and Charlie.

Jim had a hard time eating breakfast the next morning as Bobby was anxious to hear about what happened with Laurie the night before. Every time he'd take a bite, Bobby would ask another question. Bobby had taken a girl home, too, but seemed more interested in the romantic adventures Jim had with Laurie. Jim told him most of the details but kept some things close to his vest. There were moments he didn't even want to share with Bobby.

Turning to his friend, Jim smiled.

"I'm going to church today," he said. "We've got a lot to be thankful for."

"If you go, so will I," Bobby agreed.

They finished their coffee and went to take a bath in the horse trough. They were proud to have new clothes to wear, especially the dress boots given to them by Mrs. Spillar.

When they were dressed and ready, they saddled their horses and rode to the church.

Upon their arrival, they were greeted warmly by the folks in the congregation. This sort of warm welcome made them feel as though they'd never left to go to war. The boys found a place for themselves on a pew and settled to enjoy their first Sunday service in a while.

After welcoming everyone to God's house, Reverend Jones paid tribute to all of those who'd lost their lives while defending the town. He then spoke of all the people who had defended their friends and neighbors so valiantly. Finally, he mentioned the courageous efforts Jim and Bobby made to bring the army to Mexia's rescue.

The boys sat squirming with embarrassment, but at the same time, it felt good to be appreciated.

As the reverend continued with announcing church-related events, Jim couldn't help but look for Laurie. It didn't take long to spot her. She sat in the front of the congregation with her parents and little brother and sister. At that moment, Laurie looked quickly back at Jim. She was discreet as she could be, not wanting her parents to see her stealing glances.

After a while, her little brother started pestering her by poking her and then looking back at Jim to laugh.

Thankfully, the reverend started the sermon and her little brother turned to the front and left Laurie alone. The reverend's sermon was aptly titled "Thou Shalt Not

Kill," a subject covered by the Sixth Commandment. The congregation sat glued in their seats, spellbound by the words that were so appropriate considering what they had just experienced.

It was a hard message for Jim, as he had a difficult time reconciling killing fellow human beings and being a good Christian.

"There are times when a humble and gentle person must transform his plow into a sword and do what he must to protect himself, his family and neighbors. We have just come through one of these times when he had to take up arms to protect our property and our loved ones. We do not take pride in these things, but we also do not condemn ourselves for them, either."

The words spoke powerfully to Jim and had some effect on the confusion he was feeling. He was grateful that he been there to witness such a powerful sermon and hear the words God meant especially for him and the people of Mexia that morning.

After the sermon, Jim made his way to the front of the congregation and made a point to engage Laurie's mother in conversation. Mrs. Pruitt was a schoolteacher and Mr. Pruitt owned one of the general stores in Mexia.

After exchanging pleasantries, the conversation turned to Laurie, with her parents stating their immediate plans for her was a college education so she could teach school like her mother.

"In frontier communities like Mexia, a college education isn't a prerequisite for teaching school, but will help earn her more money and rise to administration more quickly," explained Mrs. Pruitt.

"Where are you planning to send her to college?" Jim asked, holding his breath a bit.

"Tehuacana has a small but excellent institution of higher learning," Mrs. Pruitt answered. "I hope that Laurie will attend there."

"I've completed the tenth grade with only one year left to complete high school," Jim said, "but my folks moved from Arkansas to Mississippi. I didn't want to go back to Mississippi, so I came to Texas. I'm not bad in reading, writing, and numbers."

Mrs. Pruitt smiled and nodded her head politely.

"There's something else I'd like to speak to you about, Mrs. Pruitt," Jim said nervously. "I know I've only known Laurie for a short time, but I feel I've known her my whole life. You should be proud. She is a wonderful person. I appreciate you letting me drive her home the other night."

Jim took a deep breath and looked Mrs. Pruitt in the eyes.

"Neither one of us has been on a real date before," he continued, "but we have, with your and Mr. Pruitt's permission, made a date for Saturday night. I hope you don't think we're moving too fast. I just think she's a wonderful girl."

It was at that moment that Mr. Pruitt walked up to his wife and Jim, returning from speaking to other men in the churchyard. After shaking Jim's hand and letting him know how grateful was for the heroic efforts he had made, he turned to his wife, sensing he had interrupted something important.

"Jim has just asked if he might take Laurie on a date this Saturday night," she explained carefully.

A bit taken aback by the idea of his daughter going on a date with anyone, he breathed a deep sigh. Like any reasonable father, he knew that this day would come.

"Just take care of my little girl," Mr. Pruitt said, shaking Jim's hand. "She means so much to her mother and me."

"I appreciate your trust, sir," Jim said sincerely. "I will take good care of her by treating her with reverence and respect."

"I believe you will," Mr. Pruitt said approvingly.

After church, Jim rode Charlie home as though they were floating on air. It was a wonderful day.

Later that evening, Jim and Charlie rode out on the range to gather as many scattered cattle as possible to bring them in for a count. Mr. Spillar was never sure of the number of cattle on the ranch since some were always missed at round-up. This time, they were especially careful to count as they wanted to make sure a portion of the large herd hadn't been killed during the Indian raids.

After counting, it appeared that only a few had been slaughtered for food. Indians usually preferred buffalo meat, which was in short supply in this part of Texas. It took a lot of meat to sate the number of Indians on the recent raid.

They spent most of Sunday riding over the entire ranch until Mr. Spillar was satisfied most of his herd was still intact. His horses were in the corrals near the barns, except the few taken during the raids.

"Don't you think we should check for our brands on the horses we confiscated from the Indians?" Jim asked Mr. Spillar. "We might find some of our horses in their herd. The other ranchers and stockmen should have the same opportunity. Even if we don't find their lost horses, they should still take what they can use. I guess I'm just a softie, but hate to see good horses killed. Most of those horses appear to be well-bred. Those Indians only ride the best horses."

"Jim, you've got a good head on your shoulders," Mr. Pruitt smiled. "I think you'll make a good cowman."

"Thank you, sir," Jim said, blushing. Mr. Pruitt's opinion of him was especially important now.

"Yes, he will," Mr. Spillar agreed. "If you don't mind my intruding, Jim, what are your future plans? Both you and Bobby can have a job on my ranch as long as you want."

"I honestly don't know, Mr. Spillar," Jim replied. "It all depends on the war."

Mr. Spillar nodded as they rode next to each other.

"Bobby told me talked with a trooper the first day we came back through Teague," Jim continued. "He was in the 10th regiment, like us, but from a different company. He had escaped by just walking away before we were put into the boats. It wasn't too hard to do, I guess. I heard a lot of men on the fringe of the battle lines just faded back into the trees and kept walking. After he procured a horse, he got back home pretty quickly. I never did ask him what 'procure' meant."

Mr. Spillar listened intently, anxious to know what the man had said.

"He said he'd been told that our old regimental commander, Colonel Nelson, was attempting to raise another military unit to go back and fight in the war. I don't want to go back, but I feel it is my moral obligation to do so. I won't go looking all over the country for them, but if they get organized and go back to battle, I will, too."

"I understand," Mr. Spillar responded. "That, it seems, is the right thing to do."

"For the time being, though," Jim told him, "I'm going to work for the Spillar Ranch, wear decent clothes, and eat and sleep as well as I can. I've also met a young lady and I'd hate to leave Mexia until I get to know her better."

"That makes good sense," Mr. Spillar said.

For a while, the men rode in silence, until Mr. Spillar turned to Jim with a solemn look on his face.

"Something I didn't tell you, Jim," Mr. Spillar began. "We lost our boy, Bill, to disease at the Little Rock General Hospital. I know you worked on the ranch together, but he didn't join the rest of the boys at Fairfield like you did. He was a member of Company D, if I remember correctly."

"I knew him here at the ranch," Jim replied, "but he was a Spillar and we cowhands didn't much associate with the boss' family. I got to know him better in the army. He came down with the measles and that's when they transferred him to a hospital. I had no idea he passed away. I'm so sorry."

"Thank you," Mr. Spillar said. "I'm just glad he had someone he knew with him when he became ill. It has been very hard on his mother."

Just then, the other cowhands began to arrive.

"We'll talk about this later," Mr. Spillar told Jim. "His mother might like to be involved in the discussion."

"Whatever is appropriate, Mr. Spillar," Jim replied. "I owe so much to your family."

"We feel that you and Bobby are part of our family," Mr. Spillar said. "Especially you."

As Mr. Spillar turned and rode to meet the cowhands, Bobby rode up next to Jim.

"What are you thinking about, Jim?" Bobby asked with curiosity. "You look like you're deep in thought."

"Mr. Spillar just told me that his son, Bill, died of measles in a Little Rock hospital after he left the camp. You remember him, I know."

"I knew he had some sort of disease, but I didn't think it was that serious," Bobby replied sadly.

"You know they've already lost two sons in war, and now Bill. It's a hard life in a hard country," Jim said thoughtfully. "The women have to be as hard and tough as the men and sometimes I feel they're tougher. Look at Mrs. Spillar and what she's been through. Mr. Spillar said it's awful hard on her, but she keeps pushing forward."

Bobby nodded in agreement. Mrs. Spillar was one of the strongest people he'd known.

After a few minutes of quiet reflection, Jim spoke.

"Are you going back if another regiment is formed?" He asked.

Bobby turned to look Jim in the eye.

"I don't know," he replied. "I may go back, but right now I'm going home to Columbia to see my folks. I haven't seen them in three years and don't even know it they're still alive. I know they haven't been able to get mail in a long time and neither one of them is any good at writing letters."

Jim nodded. He knew Bobby missed his family a great deal.

"If everything's in shape at the farm," Bobby continued, "then I'll come on back. If another regiment is formed, I'll go with you, if you're still here. If you've already gone, I'll catch up."

Bobby looked at Jim solemnly.

"Going home is something I've got to do," Bobby said. "I hope you understand."

"I do understand," Jim replied. "I know seeing your family means a lot."

"Thanks, Jim," Bobby said with a heartfelt nod. "It will mean a lot to everybody at home, too, I know."

"You should tell Mr. Spillar as soon as possible so he can assign someone else to your rotation," Jim told him.

"You're right," Bobby replied. "I'll tell him right after supper tonight."

The world was moving swiftly for both boys. They were now men in age and experience. Though they were both only twenty years of age, they had already spent three years in the army, fought Missouri Red Legs, Mexican raiders, and Comanche Indians. They had even escaped capture on the Mississippi and set out to find a battalion to help their adopted town. It seemed they had lived the lives of a hundred men in only a short amount of time.

After Bobby left for home, Jim' ranch work went well and he often rode over to the Pruitt home to visit Laurie when she was out of school. Mr. Spillar was gradually increasing his workload and paying him a little extra at the end of the month for his hard work. At Laurie's house, he had been getting on well with both her parents and Mr. Pruitt began to see him as a trusted member of the family.

Jim was happy but wished he could see his family in Mississippi. He loved them dearly and missed them a lot. If he had to be away from them, though, he knew his life in Mexia was a good one. In addition to his afternoon visits, he was seeing Laurie every Saturday and invited for Sunday dinner with her family almost every week. Yes, he missed his family, but was grateful for all the wonderful people who surrounded him. Life wasn't perfect, but it was good.

19

HONOR WINS

One afternoon while Jim was branding some new calves, one of the younger Spillar children rode out to meet him.

"Jim," the boy said eagerly, "You're needed at the house!"

Jim nodded to the child and wondered what the excitement was about.

"You men continue here," Jim told his fellow cowhands, "and I'll be back as soon as I can."

With that, Jim rode Charlie back to the main house, following the Spillar child all the way. As they got closer, he noticed several unfamiliar horses tied to the hitching rail. A bit anxious, he climbed the steps up the porch and knocked on the door. Mrs. Spillar opened the door and ushered him into the big family room.

Once inside, Jim saw three men in military uniforms who turned to look at him immediately. Standing, they each shook his hand and nodded hello. Jim recognized one of them as Colonel Nelson, the commander of his old regiment. As a matter of fact, the 10th had been known as Nelson's Regiment.

It turned out that Colonel Nelson was an old friend of Mr. Spillar and had come by for a visit. Mr. Spillar had told him about Jim and Bobby's escape after Arkansas Post and their brave trek back to his ranch. Jim did not know the colonel personally because of their difference in rank.

"What are your plans concerning your military obligation?" Colonel Nelson asked Jim pointedly.

"I intend to go back, sir," Jim replied, "if another regiment is formed."

"That's what I'm working on now," the colonel replied. "I'm notifying men such as yourself that you are needed to carry on the fight."

"What is the state of the army now?" Jim asked with interest. "It seems the southern armies have not had much good news since the High Tide of the Confederacy. Our defeats at Gettysburg and Vicksburg makes us wonder about our chance of success. I don't mean to sound like a man who doesn't love his country, but I love it more than ever. I just hope it's not a doomed cause with all those kids out there dying for nothing. Everyone on the battlefield is saying it's a rich man's war and a poor man's fight. Is there any truth to that statement?"

Colonel Nelson was taken aback by Jim's directness and, for a moment, didn't know what to say.

"You're a smart man, son," the colonel told Jim, recovering quickly. "I can see you are aware the chance of a quick victory is slipping away. I'm not going to shoot someone who chooses not to rejoin, but I will continue to fight because that's the honorable thing to do and I am an honorable man."

"That's the reason I'm going back to the regiment," Jim said, looking Colonel Nelson square in the eye. "Because it's the honorable thing to do."

"Thank you, son," Colonel Nelson said, shaking Jim's hand again. "The south will have a better chance with a man like you fighting for our side."

"Is there a staging area where men can come and sign up?" Jim asked.

"Yes," Colonel Nelson replied. "It's the same building where they signed up the first time. Do you remember? It's in Fairfield."

"I remember well," Jim said, pausing for a moment. "I will probably not have the youthful enthusiasm I did when I signed up the first time."

"That is to be expected," Colonel Nelson said, "but I need more mature and serious soldiers like yourself. Would you be interested in serving as Second Lieutenant in our army?"

Jim was surprised by the offer but considered it carefully.

"I would be honored to serve in that position, sir," Jim answered respectfully.

Jim knew a commissioned officer would stand a better chance in the future, especially when the time came to ask the Pruitts for Laurie's hand in marriage. If Jim did what he had been considering, that time would arrive in a few short days. He knew he wanted to ask for her hand in marriage before he left for the service. He couldn't help but think it seemed selfish, but he wanted a little happiness for himself and Laurie after the trials they'd been through in previous years. Between the war and Indian raids, sadness and fear had overwhelmed them, but he knew their union would lift the two to a special place shared by two people deeply in love. Just knowing someone else had the same love and devotion they had for each other would bring happiness even in the darkest times. As the thoughts rolled through his head, Jim cemented his plan to ask Laurie to become his wife before riding over to Fairfield on Monday.

If she accepted, it would be a short honeymoon, but short was better than none. He asked Mr. Spillar for a day off so he could go over and speak with Laurie and Mr. Spillar agreed.

On his way to see Laurie, Jim carefully considered his plans. As far as supporting his new bride, he could offer her more money and benefits as a commissioned officer than he could as a common soldier. He couldn't believe everything was happening so fast and couldn't help but a feel a bit nervous as he neared her house. Within a week, Jim could be a second lieutenant of a newly formed regiment with a beautiful new wife to boot! His head spun with the possibilities!

Because Laurie was still in high school, Jim went to see her there. In a few weeks, she would graduate and have her certification to teach in the public-school system.

As he came in sight of the school, Jim dismounted Charlie and tied her to a hitching rail. It was something he didn't have to do, because Charlie would never stray too far from Jim. He guessed it was something he did just out of habit.

When he got to the top of the steps outside the school, he paused. Taking a minute to consider his appearance, he brushed the knees of his pants with his hands and straightened his collar. When he thought he was as presentable as could be at that moment, he slowly turned the schoolhouse door.

When she heard the door begin to creak open, the teacher looked to see Jim standing sheepishly in the doorway.

"How may I help you?" She asked, a bit flustered that someone had disrupted her lesson.

"Please excuse my interruption, ma'am," Jim said, removing his hat. "I need to speak with Laurie Pruitt if you will allow it."

"Very well," the teacher said, gesturing Laurie to talk to Jim outside.

When they got outside, Laurie was worried as could be.

"What's wrong, Jim?" She asked, her eyes flashing with concern. "Has something happened to my parents? Or my siblings? What's going on?"

"Shh, shh, now, Laurie," Jim said, trying to calm her as best he could. "Everyone is just fine. I came here because I need to talk to you."

"What?" Laurie said, barely masking the irritation in her voice. "Everyone is fine? So, you think it's alright just to come and pull me from my lessons because you need to talk to me? You scared me out of my wits, Jim Walker."

"I'm going back in the army!" Jim blurted as Laurie stepped back in surprise. "My former commander, Colonel Newton, is putting together another regiment and I'm going to join up."

Laurie couldn't hide the anguish that washed over her face.

"Why?" She asked, holding back tears. "I thought we had a future right here in Mexia working for Mr. Spillar or maybe my dad."

"Laurie, I love you more than anything, but I have a moral obligation to fulfill my commitment to the army. I don't think you'd think much of me if I didn't do the honorable thing," Jim said, looking into her eyes. "Sometimes honor is the only thing a man can be proud of."

"But, Jim…" she started.

"Colonel Nelson has offered me a commission as a Second Lieutenant. Do you know how much that will mean to us once I get out? I love you so much, but even the colonel said he didn't think the South could hold out much longer."

Laurie was a bit numb as she tried to process everything Jim had said. Her daze turned to surprise, though, as Jim continued to speak.

"There's just one more thing, Laurie. I hope you'll think it's a good enough reason to pull you out of class."

"What is it, Jim?" She said, looking up into his eyes.

"Well, I just came here to see if you'd marry me, Laurie Pruitt." He said, his cheeks so red he could've sworn he had a fever.

Laurie's knees almost gave out from under her as the words came off his lips. He grabbed her and held her tight.

"Well, will ya?" He asked again, knowing full well what she would answer.

"Yes, Jim! Yes!" She exclaimed joyously. "Being your wife would make me the happiest girl in the whole world!"

Laurie was the happiest he'd ever seen her. With pure elation, he lifted her feet from the ground and spun her around. When he put her back down, they shared a quick kiss.

"But how, Jim?" She asked, her wide eyes fixed on his. "How will we make this work?"

"Well, the way I've got it figured, we'll get the permission of your parents and hopefully get married on Saturday night. That'll give us enough time to have a short honeymoon for a couple of days before I leave for the army."

Jim stood back a bit and looked to the ground.

"I've thought about this being selfish on my part," Jim said sheepishly. "but I know I could whip the whole Yankee army if I knew you were home waiting for me."

Laurie beamed.

"We've got to get started as soon as possible. Can you get permission to get out of school for the rest of the day?" Jim asked. "We need to check on the minister's schedule and see about the availability of the church. Also, we better talk to your parents immediately, so it doesn't appear we're doing this behind their backs. And another thing – even though you may need to take a couple of days off of school to get this done, you will be finishing school!"

"Yes, of course!" Laurie agreed, happily catching her breath. "Oh, Jim, I'm so excited! Every day since I've met you has been so wonderful!"

"Go tell your teacher you're going to be absent a few days and then we'll go talk to your parents!"

With that, Laurie disappeared back into the schoolhouse for a few minutes.

When she came out, Jim had already mounted Charlie.

"We're going to have to hurry if we're going to meet these deadlines," Laurie said hurriedly. "Now please remove your foot?"

Jim slid his food from the left stirrup, and she placed hers in it so she could swing herself up behind him.

"Let's go!" She cried excitedly. "I think it'd be a good idea to talk my parents first, if that's alright with you?"

"Yes, I think we should," Jim agreed. "You know, talking to your parents isn't something I'm looking forward to. It hasn't been that long since I asked your dad to let me take you home from the convention center."

Laurie laughed softly.

"Some day we'll have a daughter who some young man will come courting. I know I'd certainly have a hard time thinking anyone would be good enough to fancy my daughter."

"Oh, I hope so, Jim," Laurie replied dreamily. "Do you want me to go in and talk to them first?"

"No, I think we'd best do this together," he replied. "If we're going to be a team, we might as well start acting like one."

When they arrived at the Pruitt place, Mrs. Pruitt home but Mr. Pruitt was still working in town. Laurie decided not to wait to tell her mother, in hopes of having help when breaking the news to her father.

Much to the surprise of both Jim and Laurie, Mrs. Pruitt didn't seem a bit surprised to learn the two were to be married soon. In fact, she warmed to the idea quickly.

"We suspected something was brewing between you two," Mrs. Pruitt told them with a smile. "We had hoped that Laurie would finish school and gone on to college before she was married."

"We have decided she will not quit school," Jim said quickly. "Hopefully she will be able to live here after we're married since I'll be away in the army. I've been offered a commission as a Second Lieutenant and that should help us when I get back. I'm really wishing the war would end before the school year is out so we can start our new life without having to worry about my military obligations."

"Have you gotten in touch with the pastor yet?" Mrs. Pruitt asked, considering all the things they needed to get done.

"No," Laurie replied. "That's our next stop."

"We'd better hurry to him before he schedules something else," Jim said anxiously.

"You kids go on and hurry to the pastor's home and I'll tell your father," Mrs. Pruitt said, waving them on.

"Oh, mother! Would you?" Laurie exclaimed. "I was dreading telling Daddy so much! I love you more than you'll ever know!"

"Thank you, ma'am," Jim said, breathing a sigh of relief. He was grateful he didn't have to face Mr. Pruitt when he learned his baby girl was getting married.

"Now, Laurie, you two go out and get the buggy or you saddle your own horse. Riding behind Jim is not ladylike, and you're not married yet," Mrs. Pruitt told them as they prepared to go.

The two agreed and went to the coral to find Laurie's horse. Old Braze was there and came when Laurie called. She put on his bridle and saddle and mounted him with ease, showing her skill as a champion rider. Old Braze was a five-year-old blaze-faced gelding that Laurie had raised from birth. She could put her riding skills against any boy in the area.

After the short ride to the minister's house, the two noticed the minister just arriving home from an appointment.

"Hello, reverend," Jim called. "if it's not any bother, I'm wondering if Laurie and I might have a minute to speak with you."

"Of course, children," the minister replied. "It's my job to help the people of this town. Why don't you hitch your horses and come inside?"

After hitching their horses and going inside his home, the minister offered them chairs so they could sit and talk.

"What's on your minds?" He asked, looking intently at the two.

"We want to get married and we want you to perform the ceremony! What do you think, reverend? Will you marry Jim and me?" Laurie blurted, not being able to control her excitement.

"I see," replied the minister.

"We want it to be a Christian ceremony and hope it can be held in your church!" Laurie continued, barely stopping to take a breath.

"The church is not mine," the reverend replied. "It belongs to the Lord. When do you plan to have your wedding?"

"Saturday night, if possible," Laurie replied. "You see, Jim is scheduled to be reinstated with 10th Regiment and leave next Wednesday."

"Have you talked it over with your parents?" The reverend asked.

"Yes, we have," Laurie answered. "Though they wish the circumstances were different, they understand. I'm going to continue to live with them and attend school until the war is over."

"Jim, you haven't said anything," the reverend said. "Is this something you want, too?

"Oh, yes sir," Jim replied, jumping to his feet. "I've found a girl who has a good head on her shoulders and can make sound decisions on the fly. Plus, I love her."

The reverend laughed softly to himself.

"Well, Jim, I've come to discover that many successful men have a smart wife and a smart husband who listens to her," the reverend said with a smile still on his face. "Ordinarily, I would require a young couple to attend a counseling class before making such an important decision, but I understand the time restraint of your situation. Though it's happened quickly, you both seem to know what you're doing. The quantity of years in your age are just numbers. It's the caring you have for each other that's important. Never go to sleep each night without telling the other you love them."

Jim sat down next to Laurie, looking in her eyes and clasping her hand.

"You said you would like to hold the ceremony on Saturday night?" The reverend asked.

"Oh, yes. If that's alright with you, sir," Jim replied anxiously.

"Next Saturday should work just fine," the reverend replied. "Now, Laurie, how old are you?"

"I'll be eighteen next month," Laurie answered. "Will I need some sort of consent form signed by my parents?"

"Maybe in New York or Boston, but not in a frontier settlement like this," the reverend said, his eyes smiling.

"What else do we need to do?" Jim asked excitedly.

"Well, I think we need to talk to your parents, Laurie, and to the Spillars on your behalf, Jim," the reverend answered.

"I'd like to go see the Spillars first to give my dad some extra time to get used to the idea of us getting married, if that's OK with you, reverend," Laurie said.

"That's fine with me," the reverend answered as he ushered them to the door.

Outside, they mounted their horses and started toward the Spillar Ranch. Once there, they rode up to the main house, walked up the steps, and knocked on the front door.

One of the younger Spillar children answered the door.

"Mom! Dad! Its Jim and some girl!" The young boy hollered at the top of his lungs.

Soon, Mrs. Spillar was standing in the door frame.

"Jim! Laurie! It's so good to see you both," she said smiling. "We've just sat down for supper and we've got plenty. Won't you give us the honor of joining us?"

Jim looked at Laurie and she looked back at him.

"Um, Mrs. Spillar," Jim said with a serious look on his face. "Laurie and I need to speak to you and Mr. Spillar."

"Of course, he's in the dining room," Mrs. Spillar said assuredly.

Laurie and Jim followed Mrs. Spillar into the house where they saw the big table filled with kids and happy faces.

Mr. Spillar rose from the table to greet his unexpected guests.

"Ah, hello, Jim and Laurie! How nice to see you! Jim, I knew you had a good head on your shoulders and having Laurie as a friend proves it! We've known Miss Laurie all her life and she is a wonderful person!"

"Thank you, Mr. Spillar," Laurie said, blushing.

"Mr. Spillar, we need to speak to you and Mrs. Spillar. It's important," Jim started.

"Of course, Jim. We'd be happy to talk to you. Let's sit down and enjoy dinner first and then Mrs. Spillar and I can speak to afterward, when it's quieter."

"Thank you, Mr. Spillar," Jim said, sitting down at the table.

After enjoying a wonderful meal, the Spillars invited Jim and Laurie to sit with them on the porch outside.

"Now, what would you two like to talk to us about?" Mr. Spillar asked leaning back in his chair.

"Well, it's about an important decision we have to make," Jim started. "You see, since my parents are back in Mississippi, I kind of think of both you and Mrs. Spillar as my adopted parents."

"And we think of you as a son, Jim," Mrs. Spillar interjected.

"That's right, we do," Mr. Spillar agreed.

"Thank you," Jim replied. "Well, you see, Laurie and me are going to be married on Saturday night. It's not going to be a big wedding, but we would like to ask you, Mr. Spillar, to be my best man, and you, Mrs. Spillar, to be Laurie's matron of honor."

Though the Spillars were noticeably startled, they recovered quickly.

"Why, we'd be honored," Mrs. Spillar answered, her eyes filling with tears.

"We'll marry on Saturday night, so we have time for a short honeymoon before I rejoin the army on Wednesday," Jim explained. "We plan for Laurie to live with her parents while she finishes school."

Jim looked to Laurie and she squeezed his hand.

"I hope for the war to be over soon, but it's not looking good for the Southern cause. Since I'll be a commissioned officer, I'll have extra pay and benefits that will help me support Laurie, too. Of course, I'm not sure how much the Confederate money will help, once this is all said and done," Jim chuckled.

"We're proud of you two," Mr. Spillar said sincerely.

"Thank you, Mr. Spillar," Jim said, shaking his hand.

The Spillars saw Jim and Laurie to the door and said their goodbyes. Then it was time to take Laurie home.

The ride from the Spillar to the Pruitt home was quiet. Neither knew what to expect when they arrived.

As they neared Laurie's house, they saw her father in the front yard. Laurie squeezed Jim's arm a bit and he patted her hand reassuringly.

"Jim, you and Laurie come on into the house! I need to talk to both of you," Laurie's father called across the yard.

They tied their horse to the hitching rail and walked into the house, with Laurie walking nervously behind Jim.

"I understand from my wife that you two are planning on getting married," Mr. Pruitt said before anyone had a chance to sit down.

"Not without your permission and blessing, sir," Jim said.

"If we're going to lose our daughter to someone, we're both glad it's you," Mr. Pruitt said, a wide smile spreading across his face.

He reached out to shake Jim's hand and then motioned for everyone to take a seat in the living room.

"We wish you had more time to do these things, but it seems you don't," Mr. Pruitt said. "I understand Laurie is to continue living with us while you're in the service. Is that right?"

"Yes sir, we want her to finish school while I'm away. Of course, this isn't the way we wanted it to be, but the circumstances dictated our timetable," Jim replied. "We really appreciate you being so understanding. I love you both as though you were my own parents."

"Where are your parents, Jim?" Mr. Pruitt asked, leaning back into his chair. "Will they be at the wedding?"

"No, sir. They live in Mississippi and I have not seen them in over four years," Jim replied. "I love them very much, but the distance and war make it impossible for them to be present. The Northern forces occupy where they live, so visiting would be very dangerous."

"I hope this war will be over soon," Mr. Pruitt said, shaking his head. "It was only supposed to have lasted a few weeks."

"Yes, sir," Jim agreed. "I hope to introduce Laurie to them sometime soon."

"Well, it's Thursday night. You two have a lot to do before Saturday. It's best you both get some rest," Mr. Pruitt said, standing up.

Jim rose to his feet and Mr. Pruitt shook his hand once more. Mrs. Pruitt embraced him with tears in her eyes.

Turning to Laurie, Jim placed a light kiss on her forehead. It was a bit strange for both to show affection in front of Laurie's parents like that, but they were to be married soon.

"We're glad to have you in the family," Mr. Pruitt said as Jim walked outside.

On the ride home, Jim was about as happy as he'd ever been. He suddenly felt complete, not even realizing he'd been incomplete before. It all started with him thinking he wasn't good enough for Laurie to her consenting to be his wife.

God is good, he thought as he rode. *God is very good.*

The next morning, as Jim headed to the cook shack for breakfast, Mr. Spillar called him over.

"If you have something to do for the wedding, son, just take off and do it," Mr. Spillar said, putting his arm on Jim's shoulder.

"No, I think everything is done that we can do for right now," Jim answered. "I'd like to work on the ranch while I can still can."

After breakfast, Jim rode out with two other cowboys to do some branding, fix some patches in the fence, and change out some leathers on a couple of windmills. Though he enjoyed the work, it was difficult to concentrate on anything but Laurie, the wedding, and the life they would soon share together.

Between the daydreams of wedded bliss, thoughts of returning to the military crept in. He really didn't want to go. He wondered about Bobby, too. He hadn't heard from him in a long time. He prayed Bobby's parents were OK and had not met with misfortune. There was no way to contact him or his parents in West Columbia. It was too far from Mexia. Bobby was the best friend he'd ever had and worried about his safety.

Once the chores were done for the day, Jim rode over to the Pruitts to see Laurie. She had spent the day in school and just returned home.

"I know I told the teacher I was going to be absent," Laurie told Jim, "but I just needed something to occupy my mind. I'm so excited I can't eat or sleep and all I think about is you and our life together."

"I know," Jim replied. "All I can think of is the most beautiful, gracious, and intellectually gifted girl in the world and how she is going to be all mine tomorrow night. I have to pinch myself to make sure I'm not dreaming."

That evening, Jim stayed late talking to Laurie's parents. It was a pleasant visit. They all enjoyed getting to know each other. Jim thought they were wonderful people and was happy they seemed to like and accept him.

That night, after leaving the Pruitts' home, Jim rode Charlie across a prairie far from the ranch house. There, he worshipped God in his natural cathedral with the full moon and every star in the heavens shining.

Thank you for blessing me, Lord, Jim prayed silently, *undeserving as I may be. God is good.*

Saturday finally arrived and Jim spent most of his day bathing, shaving, getting a haircut and making sure his clothes would fit. Mrs. Spillar had come up with a real suit and tie and even some socks and Sunday shoes.

When he was ready, he looked like a real slicker with all his Sunday-go-to-meeting clothes. He couldn't help but feel pretty special…and just a little bit scared.

20

MARRIAGE AND BOBBY

Mrs. Pruitt still had her wedding gown and with a little taking up and letting out, it fit Laurie just fine. Laurie was so excited to be married in her mother's gown. She and Jim didn't expect much of a crowd, just close relatives and a few family friends. During the ceremony, however, they were surprised to see that the church was standing room only. Jim had saved some money from working on the ranch to buy Laurie a simple wedding ring. Mr. Spillar was there to act as best man and Mrs. Spillar was there to act as matron of honor. As they walked down the aisle, Jim noticed a friendly face in the crowd. It was his best friend, Bobby.

Thank you, God, Jim silently prayed as he stood at the altar. *Everything is right with the world.*

The ceremony was over quickly and it seemed every man in the state of Texas shook Jim's hand and kissed Laurie on the cheek.

"You're not good enough for her," the men would laugh.

Jim laughed, too, and secretly thought they were right.

The last person in line was Bobby, who apologized for not having gotten back sooner.

"I'm sorry, Jim," Bobby told him. "My parents needed my help and I'm not convinced I'll go back into the army again."

Jim told him that Colonel Nelson had visited and was recruiting for a new regiment.

"He offered me a commission if I go back in for the duration, so I agreed to go back," Jim said. "I know the South has no chance of winning, but to me, it's just a matter of honor. Being an officer will help me better take care of Laurie, too. I bet he'd give you the same opportunity if you signed up again."

"I'm not sure," Bobby said. "I've given three years to the military and I don't think we have a chance of winning. I feel that I've already fulfilled my commitment and you have, too. For now, I'm going to stay in the bunkhouse at the ranch and try to figure out what to do."

Mr. Spillar had already told Bobby that he could have his old job back or at least stay at the ranch until he decided what to do.

As for Jim and Laurie, they soon rode off in a buggy furnished by her parents that had a large "Just Married" sign on the back and strings of tin cans trailing behind.

The Pruitts' had a mother-in-law house behind their main house which was used by Mrs. Pruitt's mother until she passed away. This was to be Jim and Laurie's honeymoon cottage and they were grateful for it. The first night they spent there was blissful and it was so wonderful to finally be able to hold each other in the other's arms.

The next morning, they got up and had breakfast in time to make it to Sunday school. When the time came, Jim and Laurie both answered the invitation and rededicated their lives to God. Jim had been saved at a young age back in Mississippi and Laurie had been saved when she was twelve years old. They both felt it was good, however, to start fresh again together.

After the church service, the Spillars invited everyone out to the ranch to honor the newlyweds and wish Jim well before he went back into the service. In the main house, there was a large room especially designed for social functions and, at times, entertaining their ranch hands.

Everyone enjoyed a wonderful afternoon and it wasn't long before the time came to bid everyone goodbye. When everyone had left, Jim and Laurie climbed back into their buggy with the sign and cans trailing behind and went back to the cottage for some time to be alone. They knew their time would be limited and they wanted to make the most of the time they had left.

The next morning, a rooster crowing woke Jim as he cradled Laurie in his arms.

"I love you more today than I did yesterday and less than I will tomorrow," he said, kissing her gently on the lips.

"Just think," she said, looking up into his eyes, "when you get back from the army, we'll spend every day just like this. I love you so much."

"I've got to hurry and get over to Fairfield," Jim said sadly. "It's not something I want to do, but I'm honor bound to do it."

"I especially don't like it either, but I understand," Laurie replied, with tears in her eyes.

"I'm going to meet Bobby in front of the livery stable at nine. He's going to ride over with me and talk to Colonel Newton about going back in," Jim said. "He really doesn't want to go but he is going to go and see what Colonel Nelson has to say."

Over the next half hour, they dressed and hugged, ate and hugged, and then the time came for Jim to leave. They hugged an especially long time then. After a long, sad goodbye, Jim went out and saddled Charlie before riding toward town.

Bobby was standing beside his horse when he saw Jim riding up.

"You're early!" Bobby yelled, laughing. "Did she kick you out already?"

"She'd have to do an awful lot of kicking to get rid of me," Jim replied with a wide grin on his face.

They both laughed and mounted their horses.

"Have you decided anything about going back in?" Jim asked earnestly.

"I really haven't, but I want to see what Colonel Nelson offers me and then I'll decide," Bobby replied thoughtfully.

The twenty-minute ride to Fairfield went by fairly quickly. The whole time, Bobby told Jim about his time in West Columbia and what he was going to do if he didn't re-enlist.

Both men also reflected on how different it was when they first signed up to join the war effort. Their attitudes were completely different, as they were young and seeking glory. They had no idea about the horrors of war and the needless waste of young lives.

21

MILITARY CALLS AGAIN

"It is good that war is so horrible, for fear
that they might grow fond of it."
- Robert E. Lee

When they arrived in Fairfield, there a lot of young men standing around the courthouse. Some of them were vaguely familiar, most likely men they had served with before. Jim and Bobby dismounted and asked a couple of men where Colonel Nelson's office was located. Though the men were not sure, they thought it might be on the second floor of the courthouse.

After thanking the men, they entered the courthouse and immediately saw a sign that read "10ᵗʰ Texas Infantry, Second Floor."

"Well, I think we've found it," Bobby said after climbing the stairs.

In the back of the room sat Colonel Nelson in his Confederate uniform. When he saw Jim and Bobby, he stood and motioned them over.

"It's good to see a couple of familiar faces again," Colonel Nelson told them. "I know we did not associate with each other before, but I knew who you were and kept close tabs on as many of my enlisted men as possible. The non-fraternization rule will not be in effect particularly between Jim and me...which brings me to an important question. What are you going to do, Bobby?"

"I don't really know what to do," Bobby said, looking perplexed. "I have parents in West Columbia who are getting old and need my help. I also don't have the appetite for war that I had when I enlisted before. I feel the fortunes of war have turned against the South. Not many of the men I enlisted with are still alive and the ones that have survived are in prison camps. I must add that nobody loves the South more than I do. I've given a lot to her, as has Jim. I don't know if it gives me a right to make these statements, but I feel it's time for honest discussions."

"Bobby," the Colonel began, "they have offered you a commission as a Second Lieutenant. To be completely frank with you, I wasn't sure I would offer it to you until you just spoke your mind. The army needs officers who can think for themselves. I think you have the good sense not to give your candid opinion to anyone who will listen."

Colonel Nelson paused and looked at the men before him.

"It's lunchtime. Let's eat lunch and you can give me your decision after we've finished. Jim, I assume you're going to take your commission?"

"Yes, sir," Jim replied quickly. "I am."

"Very good. You will be assigned as platoon leader to Charlie company, or Company "C". If you decide to join,

Bobby, I will assign you as platoon leader of Company Bravo, or Company "B". Most members of your units will be men who escaped after being captured at Arkansas Post."

"I don't think I will know any of these men on a personal basis," Jim told the Colonel, "so I shouldn't have any problems with being too close with the men in my company."

While Jim and Colonel Nelson spoke, Bobby sat quietly contemplating with a serious look on his face.

"Colonel, if I can receive a commission, I'll sign up an do my best," Bobby told Colonel Nelson.

"Well, I now have all of my officer assignments fulfilled," Colonel Nelson said with a smile on his face. "We hope to have a complete compliment of troopers by next Monday. Because most of these men have served before, we won't have to spend much time on close order drills or other basic training procedures. In addition to having the ranks filled, I also would like weapons and equipment issued and have the men ready to march by next Monday. That means you must be here for reveille Saturday morning at 6 in the morning. You've got the remainder of this week to take care of any business at home and say goodbye to your loved ones."

"I don't mean for you to divulge any secrets," Jim told the Colonel, "but do you have any idea where we'll be going and what we'll be doing?"

"I'm not sure," the Colonel replied, "but I have been told that a contingent of Yankee troops was trying to link up with General George Thomas' troops at Nashville. General John Bell Hood with the Confederate army will be attempting to prevent the consolidation around Springdale or Franklin,

Tennessee. That's just southeast of the state's capital at Nashville. This is important so go home and report again Friday night or early Saturday morning for muster."

Overwhelmed with new information, Jim and Bobby bade their commander goodbye and headed for Mexia.

"What have we gotten ourselves into, Jim?" Bobby asked after they had ridden in silence for a few miles. "If what the colonel said was true, this could be a very rough campaign."

"Bobby," Jim replied. "I'm glad you'll be with me. I love you like a brother. We've been together a long time and survived some tough action, but I hope I didn't just convince you to do something that will cause you harm."

"Jim," Bobby said, "I just turned twenty-one. This decision is my own. If we survive this, it will be good for us. Anything worthwhile requires some effort and bravery."

Jim and Bobby rode the rest of the way to Mexia deep in thought. When they got to the outskirts of town, Jim asked Bobby to go home with him and share supper with himself and Laurie.

"If it's not too big an imposition," Bobby replied, "I would like that. I have no idea when I'll have the opportunity to have a home-cooked meal again. Even when I was home, my mother was ill, so I had to do my own cooking."

Once at the cottage, Laurie met them at the door and threw her arms around Jim and kissed him hard.

"Whoa, girl!" Jim said to her, pulling back a bit. "We've got company!"

Laurie looked sheepishly beyond Jim and saw Bobby standing there with a shy grin on his face.

"Bobby, please forgive me," Laurie said with a look of embarrassment on her face. "I thought we were alone."

"No, no!" Bobby said, smiling. "Forgive me! I see now why Jim is always in a hurry to get home!"

"Is it alright if Bobby has supper with us?" Jim asked his new wife. "He's agreed to join the army again, too."

"I'm glad you'll be there, Bobby," Laurie said with a sense of relief. "It will be good for Jim to have his best friend with him. You two can take care of each other."

The meal was spent visiting and talking about what life would be like when they returned home.

"Laurie, your cooking is wonderful," Bobby said with appreciation. "You are kind to accept me as a dinner guest on such short notice. I must say again – I understand why Jim is so smitten with you!"

"Don't go too far, Bobby," Laurie laughed. "You'd make a good backup for Jim!"

The next few days flew by. During that time, Bobby and Jim both wrote wills in case anything happened to them while gone. Every evening, Jim and Laurie would visit the creek where they stopped on their first date. It was a wonderful time in their lives that ended much too soon.

After graduating from high school, Laurie was to attend Tehuacana in the fall. Jim felt good that Laurie would be in the capable and caring hands of her parents while he was gone. Everyone loved Laurie.

On Friday night, Jim and Bobby left before sundown so they would have plenty of time to get to Fairfield and make the 6 a.m. reveille on Saturday morning.

Jim felt a mixture of apprehension and excitement as he bid goodbye to Laurie. He left Charlie with her and knew she would take good care of Jim's oldest friend.

Jim and Bobby arrived a little after midnight and laid their bedrolls on the courthouse lawn. Sleep was difficult due to the excitement. In the recent past, Jim had also gotten used to sleeping in a feather bed. Sleeping on the ground wasn't as exciting as he remembered it.

Jim woke up as the eastern sky lightened with the first rays of the morning sun. The smell of freshly brewed coffee was invigorating and refreshing. The company cook had a large black pot brewing the coffee. Grabbing a cupful, Jim waited for the morning wake-up call as he drank. He had almost finished his second cup of coffee when Colonel Nelson stepped out and attempted to outline some type of workable formation.

The soldiers he would be working with were farm boys and ranch hands. None of them were professional soldiers. Though they might not have had much military experience, their ability to fight was not in question. The major challenge would be teaching them organizational cohesiveness, which could only be overcome with working together over time. Time was something, though, that was in short supply.

Over the next two days, they worked hard selecting enlisted men for roles such as platoon sergeant and squad and fire team leaders. The company was woefully short of personnel, but for the time being had to work with what they had. By Monday morning, the soldiers' ability to work together had improved, though they still needed work. A lot of work.

22

MARCHING ORDERS

Monday morning after first formation, the troops marched down to the rail station and loaded aboard boxcars. These were categorized as 40x8, meaning they were big enough to carry either forty men or eight horses. In this case, there were forty men in each boxcar, and it was hot and uncomfortable for all of them.

"This may not be the most comfortable place I've ever been, but it sure beats walking," one of the men sitting close to Jim said.

Jim agreed. He knew a train ride was better, especially when he remembered his travels southward after escaping the boat on the Mississippi.

The trains stopped every couple of hours for food and pee breaks. The route was specifically selected to avoid Northern troops. On the way to their destination in Columbia, Tennessee, they were set to pass through Shreveport, Louisiana, Jackson, Mississippi, and Birmingham, Alabama.

It took them almost three days and three nights to reach Columbia, where they waited two more days for Hood's army to arrive. The weather was cold as it was deep in the fall and snow and sleet fell almost constantly. Campfires were dangerous because they could be seen from great distances. The men, all from Texas, were not used to the cold weather and suffered harshly. Late in the morning after the second day of arrival, Hood's army came tramping up the pike leading to Spring Hill.

Hood's Army did not stop when they passed Jim's unit, but kept marching as though they weren't there. It seemed that anybody who was anybody passed by them that day. The Texas unit just stood at attention as generals such as Hood, Granbury, Cleburne, and Forest came by on the pike. There were more, but those were the only ones they could recognize from their position.

Most of the troops wore clothing that was tattered and frayed with dilapidated footwear or none at all. Their spirit, however, was something to behold. They might not have been invited to a classy ball, but they had a lot of fight left in them. The dance they were headed to was being hosted by General George Henry Thomas, also known as the Rock of Chickamauga.

General George Henry Thomas was a Virginian who did not side with his native state but fought for the Union instead. He gained his nickname during the Battle of Chickamauga when he remained on the battlefield and prevented a total collapse of the Union lines. He and 30,000 of his troops would be waiting for the Confederates in Nashville.

Behind the Southern units, several thousand Union soldiers were led by General John McAllister Schofield who was trying to meet up with General Thomas' troops in Nashville. This caused quite a problem, as the Southern troops were between the forces of these two generals. It was up to the Confederate troops to make sure these two large Union groups did not link up. This was sure to lead to a difficult battle, but especially for the South.

After Jim's unit waited for General John Bell Hood's Confederate Army to pass, they fell in line and marched behind them on the pike. They arrived in Spring Hill at about nine o'clock and bedded down as best they could in the wooded area off the road. Colonel Nelson told Jim and the rest of his troops there was a Northern army coming up the road behind them, but they would post sentries and skirmishers to prevent being surprised.

Bobby and his platoon bedded down close to Jim and his troopers. Once the men were down and company guards were posted, Bobby and Jim tried to get some rest as they knew the next day would be taxing. At about two o'clock in the morning, Jim was awakened by someone shaking him.

It was Bobby.

"Wake up, Jim! Wake up!" He said hurriedly.

Very quickly, Jim was alert from a deep sleep.

"Jim, there are thousands of men marching by on the road. Are they our troops?" Bobby asked.

"I don't think so," Jim replied. "Remember we were at the end of the column this afternoon. There was nobody behind us."

"I think we should tell someone, but who?" Bobby questioned.

"We need to report it to Colonel Nelson," Jim answered. "He'll know who we should tell."

"Do you know where he is and how to get to him without being shot?" Bobby asked.

"If the entire Northern army can march by on the open highway and not be challenged, I should be alright," Jim said hopefully.

After a diligent search for Colonel Nelson, however, Jim came up empty. He couldn't find anyone with authority to take appropriate action. If the troops that passed by them were General Schofield's, a colossal mistake had been made.

It did not take them long to realize that the troops that passed them in the night were indeed Union soldiers. Now, there was nothing standing between them and their brethren in Nashville. The Confederate soldiers had allowed them to pass without any problem and there was no doubt that the coming battle would be anything less than catastrophic.

THE BATTLE OF FRANKLIN TENNESSEE YOU CAN SING OF YOUR CLEMENTINE AND YOUR ROSA LEE, BUT GENERAL HOOD OF TEXAS PLAYED HELL IN TENNESSEE

After a sleepless night, Colonel Nelson called a meeting of his officers.

"I spent last night at General Hood's headquarters," the colonel began, "and, after much discussion, have planned a form of attack. Their unit will attach to General Granbury's and attack the middle of the Yankee line near the Carter house. None of the generals who met last night were comfortable with Hood's plan, particularly not General Patrick Cleburne and General Nathan Bedford Forrest. At one point, General Forrest had to be restrained from physically attacking General Hood. Hood had accused

Forrest and Cleburne of being too scared to fight and those are two men you don't accuse of being cowardly."

The officers nodded in agreement.

General Patrick Cleburne had been at odds in the past with Hood. Hood had implied that Cleburne was a little slow to lead his men into heavy combat. He had also said the same about Forrest. Cleburne and Forrest, however, were two of the best generals in the Southern army and probably in the North or the South. Neither had attended the accepted military schools, such as West Point or VMI, which almost every military leader, whether Union or Confederate, had attended. Instead, Cleburne had been in the Irish army before coming to the United States and Forrest only had a couple years of formal schooling. Though Forrest never studied tactics at West Point, in later years, his tactics would be taught at West Point.

Before the military, Cleburne was a dentist and operated an office in Little Rock, Arkansas. Forrest was a self-made millionaire through investing and the slave trade. Both Forrest and Cleburne joined as privates and rose through the ranks. Most of the Southern army felt that Cleburne should have been at the head of the Southern Army instead of General Hood. General Forrest was promoted to Lieutenant General, but by that time, it was too late for the Southern cause.

"So, we will be attached to General Granbury's regiment and be involved in a frontal attack of what appears to be a very fortified position," Colonel Nelson continued. "Granbury has a lot of scrappy Texas boys in his unit and you might recognize some of them from back home. Write your letters and do whatever you need to do to get ready and shove off. We are scheduled to start the attack at 9:00 sharp. I'm not going to blow smoke. This battle will not be easy. Some of the boys dressed in blue are armed with repeating rifles. This is what Forrest and Cleburne were concerned about: attacking men with that much firepower behind well-fortified positions."

When the time came, Colonel Nelson attached his company to General Granbury's unit with orders to attack the center of the line. Before the battle, Bobby turned to Jim and smiled.

"I should have gone home to West Columbia!"

With that, they fell into their respective positions and headed northwest, following the order to close ranks.

The Battle of Franklin, Tennessee was nothing short of chaotic. When it was over, there were a thousand bullet holes in the Carter House alone. Except for a portion of the Northern army who were issued repeating rifles, there was no time to reload. The armies were fighting in close combat using bayonets, their rifles as clubs, and even rocks to bring the enemy down. It was unlike anything Jim had seen before.

By the time it was done, six Confederate generals, including Cleburne and Granbury, and 7,000 Southern troopers were killed.

The Yankees pulled out early the next morning and headed for Nashville to link up with General Thomas. The Southern Forces gathered the wounded, buried their dead, and created some order out of the confusion.

General Cleburne was found dead on the battlefield with his weapon, boots, and uniform taken by scavengers. It was not a fitting end to a great man.

Bobby was found at the far reaches of the battlefield within ten yards of General Granbury. He, too, was dead.

Completely heartbroken, Jim carried his friend to a large oak tree and buried him in its shade. He marked the tree so he could find it and hopefully bring Bobby back to Mexia eventually.

Though torn apart by the loss of his best friend, Jim knew he was a soldier with duties to perform. He no longer felt quite honor-bound to a lost cause, but he had a sense of obligation to his men. He had to make sure the wounded were cared for and organize those who were healthy enough to march to Nashville to meet General Thomas. It was not a meeting Jim was looking forward to. Though he was glad to be alive, he felt as most of the other troopers did – disheartened and disillusioned. The war was lost, and people were dying for no good reason. Jim, like most of the men, just wanted to go home.

When Jim counted heads, he learned that about fifty percent of his platoon was dead, wounded, or captured. Bobby's platoon was in approximately the same fix. He gathered the surviving squad leaders together and asked if they would be willing to combine their men with his to form a full-strength platoon. They agreed and fell into formation to march on to Nashville. They were heartbroken men who left their friends behind underneath cold, unfriendly sod. Tears flowed freely down their cheeks as they headed down the pike.

On the orders of Colonel Nelson, Jim and his platoon acted as a rear guard for the Southern army. He felt this was the Colonel's way of giving their unit some relief. They had been hit hard.

The leading forces were already encountering the federal defenses in Nashville. The results of this encounter would be the same they faced at Franklin except more were killed, captured, and wounded. The young men who had given so much for what was now a lost cause had once again marched into a battle with no hope of victory. It was both distressing and honorable at the same time.

Because Jim's platoon was in the rear, they were spared heavy combat. By the time they reached Nashville, the outcome was inevitable.

General Hood tendered his resignation after the battle, and it was accepted. Most of the surviving units that were still somewhat intact went on to fight for other units in the east and the south, along with Colonel Nelson. Many of the Southern troops were disillusioned with their commander and just went home.

Jim left Nashville with most of his new unit intact. He decided to go home for the second time in the war. He had a heavy heart, leaving Bobby behind in Franklin, but was anxious to get back to Texas and see Laurie. It hadn't been a long time, but it felt like a lifetime.

24

GOING HOME AGAIN

Jim offered to make the trip to fight in the Carolinas with Colonel Nelson, but the colonel declined the suggestion.

"Go home and see your wife and take care of the home front. The war will be over in less than six months."

Colonel Nelson looked down at the ground solemnly.

"Lee can't hold out much longer without food and ammunition and Johnston will encounter General Sherman on his march from the Georgia coast to Richmond," the colonel said. "It's just a matter of time. They will just need some protection from the carpetbaggers and scalawags who will show up at the end."

With some finality, Colonel Nelson looked Jim square in the eye.

"I have no idea what kind of governmental control will be instituted once the war is over. Will the high-ranking officers be considered traitors and shot? Of course, there's no question we've lost the war, but how will be treated after we are defeated? That's the question."

After his talk with the colonel, Jim called his men together and explained the situation. He offered to release the men who wanted to go with the colonel and fight to the bitter end or they could march as a unit back to Mexia.

Not one man left the ranks to go with Colonel Nelson. Jim told the men they would leave at 6:00 the next morning and begin their trek back to Texas. Before they left, Jim did a head count and tallied about twenty-five soldiers.

They needed horses badly. Being from Texas, they were all experienced riders. They all dreaded the prospect of walking several hundred miles to get back home. Jim asked them if they were willing to help make a midnight raid on the Yankee Depot to reacquire some of their horses that had been taken. Each man volunteered enthusiastically, and a plan was made.

"In all likelihood, the horses will be lightly guarded by the men on guard duty," Jim told his troopers. "I don't expect them to be too diligent since they assume the battle is already over. We don't want to fire our guns for obvious reasons. If we make a sound, we risk the whole Yankee army coming down on us. And we don't want to hurt anyone unless we have to."

At about 10:00 that night, the troops darkened their faces and other exposed skin and marched toward the Yankee encampment. The sky was overcast, and the men had trouble seeing the men in front of them until their eyes became used to the darkened environment. They had no trouble sneaking into enemy territory, as the Yanks were enjoying the spoils of victory including some spirited drinks.

Jim with a hand signal motioned for his men to gather around him.

"The horses are just ahead," Jim said quietly, "and there are only three guards. I want the guards surprised, gagged, and tied up. I don't want anyone to be overly rough with them unless it's necessary. While some of our men are taking care of the guards, the other troops will go into the stables and saddle as many horses as possible and ride like hell to our campsite."

The men nodded their understanding.

"I don't want any of this to be discovered until the next change of guards, which will be at around 2:00 in the morning," Jim continued. "This should give us enough of a head start to keep ahead of the Yankees, who will most likely be hungover from their drinking spree."

The plan went off without a hitch and the men hurried back to their camp where they prepared to leave before mounting their newly acquired horses. They rode as hard as they could until they felt comfortable enough to stop and rest.

Though the horses were big, stout, and steady, the men agreed that they preferred the quarter horses back in Texas. The horses they rode now were more like plow horses than riding horses.

"They're like riding horses," one of the men quipped, "because they remind of riding in a rocking chair!"

The troops skirted the larger communities and stopped at the smaller southern settlements for food and water. When time for sleep came, they stopped in clumps of trees and slept in shifts. Nobody ever got more than four hours of sleep at a time. They traveled both day and night, with their biggest problem being crossing large bodies of water like the Mississippi and Arkansas rivers. Fortunately, they were able to find ferries sympathetic to the southern cause who were always willing to help them across. Though they had some Confederate money, everyone knew it was no longer worth the paper it was printed on.

After the boys left Tennessee, they traveled through Mississippi and Arkansas before finally riding into Texas. They had to be careful as there were still large Yankee contingents in this region. Luckily, the troops made it without any problems. The civilians in the areas where they stopped were more than willing to hide them, feed them, and put them up in their barns for overnight stays. They also helped the troops gauge the location of the Yankee's camps and directional movements.

Though the civilians did not treat them as conquering heroes, they were treated with sincere appreciation for all they had done. These soldiers had little need for backslapping, flag-waving, or glory. They had lived like animals while fighting in the war and simply wanted to go home and lead normal lives. Jim and his men were grateful for the kindness of the civilians and heartily thanked them for their assistance.

When they crossed into Texas at Texarkana, they began to head south toward home. By that time, the trees had lost all their leaves and the weather was cold. Even so, the boys were warmhearted and felt good about being so close to home. Several of the boys left the group in the norther part of the state since their families lived in communities like

Fort Worth, Waco, and Weatherford. As they rode their last stretch to home, the men were all filled with mixed feelings of joy and sorrow.

Jim was sorrowful because he had to leave his best friend back in Franklin. He blamed himself for Bobby's death because he put so much pressure on him to re-enlist. Jim knew he had to ride down to West Columbia and inform Bobby's parents of his death. It was not something he was looking forward to, but felt it was the least he could do.

Before riding down to see Bobby's parents, though, Jim would go to see his wife. This thought overjoyed him, and he was anxious to get home and hold Laurie in his arms again. God had been so good to allow such a woman to be his wife. He rode through Teague to the Pruitt's home, battling mixed emotions. Despite his excitement to be home, he couldn't get the thought of Bobby out of his mind.

By the time he arrived in Mexia, a misting rain mixed with sleet was falling over him. Though Laurie was still in school, she was out for the Christmas holidays. She was still living with her parents in the small house behind the main house as far as he knew. The ground was frozen and the horses' hooves made a loud thud each time they hit the ground. Jim, however, couldn't tell the sounds of the horses' hooves from his own heart pounding in his chest.

25

HOME AGAIN

Jim was excited and apprehensive, too. He was not at all the clean-cut young man that Laurie married. His clothes were ragged, his hair and beard need trimming, and he was covered in dirt from head to toe. He could have gone by the ranch and borrowed some clothes and cleaned up, but he was too anxious to see Laurie again. She was all he could think of as he rode up to the porch, tied his horse to the railing, and knocked briskly on the front door. He could hear someone walking across the floor before the door opened. When the door creaked as it swung open, Jim's stomach was tied in knots. Before him stood Mr. Pruitt.

Because of his appearance, Mr. Pruitt didn't recognized Jim at first. When Jim told him, Mr. Pruitt embraced him and pulled him inside. Then he hollered for Laurie. Mrs. Pruitt and Laurie both came running into the parlor, crying. Laurie ran and jumped into Jim's arms and kissed him as she cried. Everyone was overwhelmed with emotion. It was a special moment indeed.

"Is it really you, Jim? Is it really you?" Laurie kept asking over and over.

After everyone became more rational, they settled into the living room.

"We feared the worst as we heard of the horrific battles in Franklin and Nashville," Mr. Pruitt told Jim. "We'd heard that's where you went when you left here. We thought Laurie was a widow before she became a wife. We were so fearful."

"It was a horrible encounter," Jim said with tears rolling down his cheeks, "the worst I've ever seen. I lost over half my platoon there, including some very good friends. I hate to tell you that one of them was Bobby. I'll always feel I'm to blame as I'm the one who talked him into re-enlisting."

"No, no! Not Bobby," Laurie cried, "I loved him as a brother as I knew he was such a good friend to you!"

"I need to take a trip to West Columbia to meet with his parents and explain how he died," Jim told them. "I buried him under a large oak tree in hopes of finding him again. I intend to go back and retrieve his body after the war and bring him home for a proper burial."

"What, now?" Mr. Pruitt asked. "When do you have to go back to fight?"

"I don't think I will go back," Jim answered wearily. "The South is spent. Most of the leaders know it's over and are looking for a way to end it honorably."

Tears began to stream down Jim's face as he spoke.

"I pretty much knew it was over before the Battle of Franklin, but I wanted to be an officer and was hoping for a miracle," Jim said sadly. "What a horrible price to pay."

Laurie reached for Jim's hand and held it in her own.

"I'm sorry to talk about nothing but doom and gloom and I know I look a mess," Jim apologized. "We traveled from Nashville all the way back to Texas. We had to dodge Yankee patrols the entire way. There was no time or energy to clean up, shave, or change clothes if we even had any to change into. We're just so happy to be home and have families to welcome us when we arrived."

"Jim, take a bath in our bathroom and you can use Laurie's daddy's shaving equipment, just this once, can't he?" Mrs. Pruitt looked to her husband.

"Of course, he can!" Mr. Pruitt answered. "After that, I'm sure the kids will want to spend some time alone together."

Jim kissed Laurie again, thanked the Pruitts, and went into the bathroom. When he walked in, he saw an oversized tub with hot water that Laurie was drawing for him. While the water was heating, he shaved his face and cut his hair with a pair of scissors with Laurie's assistance. The warm water felt wonderful. It had been a long time since he'd bathed with actual soap and water.

While he was soaking in the tub, Laurie laid out a change of clothes and clean underwear on the bed. Jim was exhausted but felt energized when he saw Laurie standing next to the bed. He came into the room, grabbed her, and kissed her fully on the mouth. Finally, she had to restrain him.

"Whoa, boy," she said smiling. "We need to see Mom and Dad for a little while, eat supper, and then we'll go to our house in the back. You go talk to them while I clean up the bathroom and get started on supper, OK?"

Once Jim joined Mr. and Mrs. Pruitt, Mr. Pruitt began asking him questions about the war and Mrs. Pruitt joined Laurie to help her cook.

"Do you think the Yankee military would occupy as far south as Mexia?" Mr. Pruitt asked intently.

"Yes, I think they would," Jim replied. "They were roaming south across the Sabine and Red rivers and have battled in both Sabine Pass and Galveston. To tell the truth, there's little that stands in their way."

Mr. Pruitt leaned back, deep in thought.

"The war is over for all practical purposes. Now there's only continual dying and suffering of hapless soldiers. The generals are the ones who make the decisions to continue the conflict or quit, but they aren't in the position of the privates who are paying the price."

Jim continued to tell Mr. Pruitt everything he knew.

"The battles at Gettysburg, Vicksburg, and Chickamauga pretty much depleted the South of their fighting men. The battle of Chickamauga was technically a Southern victory, but we lost a lot of men we couldn't replace. The Yankees can replace their casualties, but the South cannot. We are running out of resources, most of all fighting men. As I've said before, it's a rich man's war, but a poor man's fight. It's a lost cause out there."

"That's an awful shame," Mr. Pruitt said, shaking his head.

"And that's not all of it," Jim continued. "Lee can't adequately feed his soldiers or arm them any longer. General

Johnston is wandering up and down the east coast, putting up a good scrap from time to time, which are doomed to have no lasting effect. What's more, General Hood has resigned as head of the Western armies. I expect the war to continue a few more months only to cause more heartache and suffering. I think it's a bad habit we've gotten into of not wanting to admit we're whipped, but we are. Some of the officers just don't want to give up their power, which is over the life and death of their men."

"What do you think our fate is as civilians?" Mr. Pruitt asked.

"All I hear is scuttlebutt, but if Lincoln has his way, we'll be welcomed back into the Union with open arms," Jim said matter-of-factly. "On the other hand, there are these fire-breathing Yankee politicians who want us to suffer. I don't quite know the answer to your question, and I don't think anyone else does, either. I do think the slaves will be freed and given the right to vote. Also, only the white men who can prove they did not take up arms against or provide comfort for the south will have rights to suffrage."

It was then Mrs. Pruitt walked into the room.

"Supper's ready," she said, smiling warmly.

Jim, who had not eaten or slept regularly for a long time, eagerly stood up and followed her into the dining room. Once at the table, he sat down rather timidly as he realized he wasn't eating at a military mess. He stood again and waited for everyone else to be seated and for the blessing to be asked.

Mr. Pruitt asked Jim to give thanks and he did in a simple but heartfelt manner. As thankful as we were, Jim was also hungry. He tried to be careful that his military eating habits didn't arise while he was eating with his wife and her family. The meal was delicious and much appreciated. As the food reached his stomach, Jim realized just how exhausted he was. Fortunately, he only dozed off once during the meal.

While the ladies were fixing supper, Mrs. Jim Jefferson Walker had slipped out and fired up the wood stove in their little house so it would be warm later.

Mrs. Walker, Jim thought, *now that has a ring to it!*

After supper, Laurie helped Jim to his feet and guided him to their little home to the rear of the main house.

"I've waited for this moment for what seems like an eternity," Jim said as they entered the cottage.

Jim sat on the bed and reached for Laurie. He then lay across the bed and passed out.

Jim did not move a muscle until 11:00 the next morning. It took a while before he even realized he was home. He fully expected to wake up in the army as he had so many nights before. He then looked across the room and saw Laurie sitting in a chair. When he remembered that he was reunited with his wife once again, he was overwhelmed.

He motioned for Laurie to come to him and apologized for his exhaustion the night before. She gently put her hand over his mouth and told how much she loved him and needed him at that moment. Jim woke and was soon in wonderland.

Their lovemaking was over much too quickly, but Laurie and Jim both wanted to stay in bed all day.

This was not to be, however, as they heard Mrs. Pruitt calling that lunch was ready.

26

END OF WAR/RECONSTRUCTION

The next few weeks were a blur. It took Jim some time to get used to civilian life again and it took time for both Jim and Laurie to get used to married life for the first time. The South had entered a period called Reconstruction, and that took everyone time to adjust to. Reconstruction was the term given to the occupation and guidance provided by the Northern armies. It was an almost unbearable arrangement for the Southern states.

The carpetbaggers and scalawags had free rein with the law authorities as they were appointed and not elected. The ultimate authority was an occupying military unit that did not want to be there. The Northern troops had little sympathy for the South, whose armies they had fought for four hard years. Most of them just wanted to go home and be with their own families. There was a segment, however, that took advantage of their power and committed dreadful acts. There was usually no one who would take action to punish these offenders.

This was a problem that existed all over the South. The men who perpetrated these acts knew they were above the law. The crimes ranged from petty theft to murder. They did as they pleased, knowing there was little chance they'd be persecuted in a court of justice.

Lieutenant General Nathan Bedford Forrest gathered a small group of men to maintain some sense of order in Memphis. The organization was called the Ku Klux Klan and the members, comprised of mostly private citizens, staged midnight raids to control the guilty parties who committed unlawful acts. The Klan was protected by the Union Army and would perform raids after midnight, cloaked in hoods. It worked well until it became corrupted by local toughs and rednecks. General Forrest served as head of the organization until it ceased to be a law enforcement organization and turned into a self-serving association that was largely racist in nature.

Jim had been home for about six months when several terrible crimes were committed around Mexia. Mr. Spillar consulted with the military commander about these incidents but was rebuffed. Having no choice, Mr. Spillar then called a meeting of local male citizens of the area. He opened the meeting by explaining their predicament and asking for ideas. After some suggestions, Jim said he had heard about General Forrest's organization in Memphis.

"Were you involved with the organization at all, Jim?" Mr. Spillar asked.

"No, sir, I have never met General Forrest," Jim replied. "I've seen him at Franklin and Nashville, but never talked to him on a personal basis. I did, however, speak with some troopers who served under him. They were under the impression that the war crimes could continue even after the major conflict had ended. They said maybe some sort of secret organization could be formed to maintain order during the occupation."

"How will it work?" Asked one of the men sitting toward the back of the room.

"Well, if someone breaks the law or is disrespectful to a woman, for example, they could expect a visit from the hooded organization in the dead of night," Jim explained. "It seems to be a workable solution to what could turn out to be a real problem."

The men in the room were impressed by Jim's knowledge and Mr. Pruitt reminded them that Jim was an officer in the Southern Army.

"These lawbreakers will be at the complete mercy of the local commanding officer," Jim continued. "Whatever happens to them will be totally at his discretion."

In 1865, the war officially ended when General Lee surrendered to General Grant at Appomattox Courthouse in Virginia. It took a couple of months to reign in the fragments of the armed forces to make the surrender complete.

The situation became worse after President Lincoln was assassinated that same year. The crime committed by the known actor, John Wilkes Booth, fueled the fire-eating politicians in the North who now had all the ammunition they needed to treat the rebel states with an iron fist. No one in the North had much sympathy for the people in the South. Jim and the other men had no idea what kind of control would be exerted by the occupying forces in Mexia.

A committee was appointed with Jim acting as the authority to organize a group and report back the following week. The group was to be responsible for taking actions against those who committed criminal acts in their town. Jim wasn't completely sure this would happen, but knew they had to be ready to protect their citizens, should it occur.

At a meeting Jim called a couple of days later, he suggested a meeting with the commander of the occupying army to let him know that a clandestine army would be formed to protect the local citizens of Mexia. The men agreed with Jim wholeheartedly.

The following week, a company of the 5th New York Calvary arrived commanded by Captain Will Jim. His unit used the convention center as their headquarters and called a town meeting to inform the citizens of what was expected of them. At the meeting, the captain seemed a reasonable person who hoped Reconstruction would soon be over so everyone could go home. He stressed that if the citizens could be reasonable, then everything would be fine.

After the meeting, Jim walked up and introduced himself to the captain and requested a private meeting. Captain Jim readily accepted the opportunity to become more familiar with the town and its citizens.

"Why not now?" Captain Jim asked Jim. "We can go up to my office and discuss things that might come up during this period."

"That would be good," Jim replied. "I think it's a good idea to acquaint ourselves as quickly as possible. I was an officer in the Confederate army and understand some of the limitations you face. Unfortunately, we've heard of the atrocities committed in other jurisdictions without fear of consequence. Though we understand the South lost the war, but we are only asking for protection of those who can't protect themselves. Being on a battlefield is one thing, but to harm and humiliate citizens is intolerable."

Jim paused before speaking again.

"We are willing to pay reparation of some sort, but we will not stand by and allow soldiers to take advantage of our people."

"I won't allow anything untoward to happen on my watch," Captain Jim said assuredly. "We will take what actions are necessary to make sure of that."

"I'm relieved you feel that way," Jim replied. "The citizens are worried, especially after hearing what they have about occupations in other areas."

"Have you considered putting together a secret organization to enforce the rules and protect your citizens?" Captain Jim. "It's not something I could knowingly condone, but if I were in your situation, I would heavily consider it. I've heard it works well in other parts of the South."

Jim was taken aback by Captain Jim' statement and overall attitude.

"Just between you and me," Jim said. "we have considered it and are willing to try it. I know it will work a lot better with supportive military leaders such as yourself, Captain Jim."

After the conversation with Captain Jim, Jim called a meeting of the town committee was called and all agreed that a protective organization should be formed.

To everyone's relief, however, the remainder of the occupation passed without incident. With Jim and Captain Jim working together, the period was nothing less than quiet and respectful on both sides.

Following the departure of the Northern troops, Jim assumed his old job with the Spillar Ranch, except now as the assistant foreman under Tom. He enjoyed his job and soon learned that Laurie was with child. This was such joyous news to the newly expectant father that his chest swelled. He continually thanked God for his blessings.

Since taking on his job, he and Laurie managed to purchase ten acres from Mr. Pruitt and began saving for a home of their own. Jim and, at times, Laurie, spent as much time as possible working to clearing their new land and plotting a spot for their new home. Life was relatively calm after Jim's previous four or five years and he loved it. Nothing could compare with the elation he felt waking up beside Laurie every morning and calling himself her husband. Soon, they had a new son who they called Joshua.

Time passed quickly and Jim spent one term as Mexia's Interim mayor after the elected mayor had a heart attack and could not fulfill his official duties. Though Jim felt it was a good experience, he was glad to get home and back to punching cattle as work.

By the time Jim was back on the ranch, he and Laurie had built their home and welcome a baby girl named Ruth. The name, like her brother's, was gleaned from the Bible and reminded Jim and Laurie every day how grateful they were for God's blessings.

In 1871, tragedy struck when an epidemic illness swept over north Texas, killing countless people, including little Joshua and his precious wife, Laurie. In his little family, only he and Ruth survived.

Jim was devastated. He did not come out of their house for many weeks. Through all the tragedy he had witnessed in the Indian battles and Civil War, nothing could compare to this heartache. Laurie had been his life. He knew he would never recover from her death and little Ruth couldn't comprehend the finality of her mother's absence.

"Where is Mommy?" Ruth asked over and over in the first few months.

"She has gone to be with Jesus," Jim would reply, not knowing if it made any sense to his little girl or not.

Of course, the Pruitts tried to help, but they were in shock as well.

He buried Joshua and Laurie beneath a giant oak tree behind their home. It was a constant reminder of all he had lost.

27

BRINGING BOBBY HOME

Jim planned to go back to work after a couple of months, but before he did, he took the trip to West Columbia as promised. He asked the Pruitts if they would watch Little Ruth while he completed some unfinished business. He felt badly about not visiting Bobby's parents earlier. It had been five years. He wasn't even sure if they were alive or not.

He had also promised to bring Bobby's body back to North Columbia. He had waited for the right time to do it, and now seemed like that time. He could take a train from Fairfield to Nashville and then onto Franklin. From there, he could rent a wagon and go on to where he had buried Bobby. He still had a crude map of the burial site that he had kept in his dilapidated uniform since the battle. He also had some money he and Laurie had saved for an emergency plus the funds they used for day-to-day living.

Jim knew nothing about transporting a body hundreds of miles and needed someone to help him with the details. He went to see Claude Johnson, the owner of the funeral home in Mexia and asked his advice. Mr. Johnson told him that if the body had been in the ground five or six years, there would be considerable decay.

"Was the body wrapped or preserved in any way?" Mr. Johnson asked.

"He was buried on the battlefield at Franklin, Tennessee," Jim replied. "I wrapped him in the only thing I had, which was an army blanket.

"Take a sleeping bag with you that will zip up and make sure to wrap the body with some kind of material that won't leak. Wrap it securely and place it in a casket or wooden box to be placed in the baggage car. You'll also want to fill the container with moth balls. That will keep the smell down and preserve the body."

Jim was grateful for the information Mr. Johnson had given him and prepared to leave for his trip. Jim took Little Ruth to his in-laws and told her he loved her very much and that her grandparents would take very good care of her while he was away. Then he caught a train at Fairfield and began his long journey to keep his promise to Bobby and himself.

It took three days to travel the distance from Fairfield to Franklin. During his journey, much of the time was spent switching and waiting for other trains to pass.

When he arrived, Franklin looked nothing like he remembered. It had been cleaned up and restored. Jim went to the sheriff's office and showed them his hand-drawn map.

"Do you remember any of the terrain or features on the map?" The deputy sheriff asked.

"I remember it was near a cotton gin and the Carter House," Jim replied. "It was where Generals Cleburne and Granbury were killed in battle."

The deputy gave him the address and directions to an historical society, where the people would be able to direct him to the exact location. As he was on foot, he asked the deputy where he could rent a wagon and team. The wagon would be necessary to transport Bobby's body back to the railway station.

The directions the deputy gave him were good and he found the historical society with little or no trouble. The lady inside was helpful and didn't ask if the body belonged to a soldier wearing a gray or blue uniform.

"The location seems to be on the south end of the Carter place. That appears to be where the fighting was most horrible."

"I think I will recognize it because I buried him under a large oak tree and carved his name in the trunk," Jim told her. "Is there anyone I need to get permission from to conduct the search and dig up the body?"

"I don't think so," she said. "However, if you are questioned, just have them come and see me. Where are you taking the body and what was his relationship to you?"

"He was my really close friend. I'm taking him home to his parents in West Columbia," Jim explained. "That's a small town in Texas approximately fifty miles southwest of Houston."

With a tear in her eye, she pointed Jim in the right direction and watched him go out the door.

Jim untied his team, climbed into the wagon and tried as best he could to follow the lady's directions. The cotton gin and Carter house were easy to locate, and the landmarks were starting to become familiar. At the crest of the small hill before him, he saw the large oak tree. He popped the reins of the back of the team of horses and they broke into a trot.

I think this is the spot, he thought to himself.

As he pulled up to the tree, he saw the crude letters he had drawn so many years before.

Just as he was getting down from the wagon, a rider on a palomino came up the hill.

"Hey, wait a minute," the rider called, "who are you and what are you doing here?"

"My name is Jim Walker, sir," Jim replied. "I was a lieutenant with the 10th Texas regiment during the battle of Franklin in November 1864. I'm keeping a promise to a friend who died in General Granbury's brigade. I buried him the morning after the battle under this tree. It still has his name carved in the trunk. Can you see it?"

"I'm a member of the Carter family," the man said. "I live in a house down the hill and to the north. The heaviest fighting in this vicinity."

"I know. I was here," Jim told him. "Our casualties were about fifty percent. It was an awful scrap."

"I'm sorry for your loss," Mr. Carter replied. "Is there anything I can do to help?"

"No, but thank you," Jim answered gratefully. "I just need to unearth his body and get him back to his parents in Texas. I do, however, appreciate your kindness."

Jim had some blankets in the wagon but not the other items he needed to transport Bobby back home. He remembered he buried his friend about three feet deep in the relatively soft dirt. He was hoping the ground was still pliable and, after only a couple of spades of dirt came up, He discovered the digging was pretty easy.

It finally hit Jim that his best friend was really so near, beneath the earth, almost in his arms once more. Unashamedly, he fell to his knees and wept with his head resting on his knees.

After composing himself and digging for about thirty minutes, his shovel struck something solid. Jim got down on his hands and knees and began to dig about the bundle with his hands. He had found his old friend. Jim was crying and digging; digging and crying.

After hauling Bobby into the wagon, he hurried back to the town and immediately found an undertaker. Jim asked him if he had any sort of wooden box or cheap casket. The undertaker said he had readymade pine boxes which they used to encase the casket as it was lowered into the ground. It would, he told Jim, be the cheapest way to go. Jim asked if he would help him wrap Bobby in a sleeping bag and lift him into the box. Then he wanted to know if there was a hardware store where he could find mothballs.

Luckily, the undertaker had a supply of mothballs and a rubber container he could fit bodies into. They put Bobby in the enclosure and zipped it up. They then placed his body in the wooden box and filled it with the mothballs. Jim could not believe his good luck, having found all the necessary goods and services in one place. The undertaker told him it was not unusual as they shipped a lot of the battle victims just as they were with Bobby.

Jim paid the undertaker, but the charges were minimal. In Franklin, there was a lot of sympathy for the fallen. Jim thanked him and drove down to the railway station to place Bobby in the baggage car. They were going home.

I hope his parents are alive, Jim thought to himself on the train, *then they can be reunited and spent the rest of eternity with him.*

The return trip was uneventful, only having to change trains twice at Little Rock and Dallas. Finally, he reached his destination of Houston where he offloaded and rented another wagon and team for the last leg of his trip to carry Bobby home.

East and West Columbia were twin settlements at the mouth of the Brazos river, where it flows into the Gulf of Mexico. Jim was aware of the area's historical significance as it is where many signers of the Texas Declaration of Independence lived. Jim didn't think he would have a lot of trouble finding the Johnson homestead in a settlement that small. However, Jim wasn't even sure if Bobby's parents were still alive.

The ride from Houston to West Columbia was pleasant and gave Jim time to reflect on his life from the time he arrived in Mexia to the present. It was springtime with the flowers blooming, the trees budding, and the wildlife running before him. He felt selfish to be so grateful and full of life with Bobby's lifeless body in the back of his wagon. He passed through the small settlements of Alvin and Angleton before crossing the Brazos river and heading into West Columbia.

Just a couple of miles past the river, he arrived at the outskirts of the settlement. Once in the middle of town, Jim pulled into a trading post, tied his team to a hitching rail and walked into the store. The woman behind the counter was friendly and her name was Mrs. Lily Thompson. She was a pretty lady with grey streaks in her blonde hair.

"Are you from West Columbia?" She asked Jim.

"No, ma'am," Jim replied. "I'm from Mexia and I'm looking for the Johnson place. I've brought their son's body back so they can all be together again."

Unfortunately, Jim learned that Bobby's parents had passed away within one month of each other. They were buried down in the town's cemetery, which wasn't far from the trading post.

"I thought you might have been the son they were looking for," she said sadly.

"No, ma'am," Jim replied. "It seems I'm too late, but I'd like to bury him in the cemetery with his parents. Is there anything I need to do to obtain permission to do that?"

"Yes," she said, "I'm the person who can help you with that. If I may ask, what happened to their son?"

Jim went on to explain that Bobby had been killed in the Battle of Franklin.

"I buried him under an oak tree there and marked the grave so I could bring him home someday," Jim explained.

"Are you telling me you went all the way back to Tennessee to bring him home so he could be near his parents?" Mrs. Thompson asked.

"He wanted to be with his mother and dad and I did everything I could to help make that possible," Jim said, eyes turned downward.

"If I remember correctly," Mrs. Thompson said with tears flowing down her face, "Mr. and Mrs. Johnson reserved a spot near themselves in the cemetery to place their son."

Mrs. Thompson then raised her voice and called for her husband to come and mind the front of the store so she could take Jim to the cemetery. The cemetery was not large as the settlement was not over fifty years of age. The markers for the Johnsons' graves were cheap and nondescript, but a place for Bobby's resting place lay beside them.

"I'll have to dig the grave myself if you can mark the correct spot," Jim told Mrs. Thompson.

"You won't have to do that yourself," Mrs. Thompson said. "They have a working group who does that for local people."

"I want to do it as a labor of love," Jim replied, tears filling his eyes. "If someone could help, it would be greatly appreciated."

"Take me back to the store, then, and I will get you some help," Mrs. Thompson said, climbing back into the wagon.

Thanks to Mrs. Thompson, the grave was dug by 2:00 in the afternoon and many of the townspeople had gathered to pay their respects. She had also contacted a local minister to conduct a religious memorial for Bobby. It was a fitting tribute to his good friend.

After the service, Jim stayed with Bobby and said his last goodbye. He sadly turned his wagon toward the store and slapped his reins down on the horse's backs and headed into town. He was willing to stay in town long enough to take care of Bobby's final business and Mrs. Thompson and the reverend were willing to help with that as well. He wanted to know if there was any money from the Johnson's homestead that could be used to purchase a proper headstone.

Jim thought a headstone which covered all three plots with Bobby's mother and dad's names on the top center and Bobby's name centered beneath them would be nice. He knew, however, that this would cost a sizeable amount. If no money was left in the equity of the home, Jim was willing to pay for it himself. Mrs. Thompson said she felt certain the money could be raised from the sale of the homestead and the pockets of local citizens. Mrs. Thompson reminded Jim that the reverend had told the people during the service that he had given his life at the Battle of Franklin, Tennessee.

Jim left, knowing that Mrs. Thompson would take care of purchasing the headstone and Bobby's final affairs. Before leaving, he gave Mrs. Thompson his address and asked her to write from time to time. He told her he was grateful for all she had done for Bobby and his family. He then climbed into his wagon and headed north toward Mexia. He had no idea what he was going to do with the rest of his life. He was a widower with a young child. His lust for life and excitement had greatly diminished since he had lost Laurie. His world was gone, but he had to keep going for Little Ruth's sake.

28

LIFE AFTER LAURIE

After turning in his rented team and wagon at Angleton, Jim boarded the train to Fairfax. As he rode, he tried to focus on his blessings. He had a good job, a beautiful little girl, and his whole life ahead of him. Though he grieved for her every day, he knew Laurie would not want him to give up. He decided to do his best to begin to function as a contributing member of society again.

On the train he had read in a newspaper about good, cheap land near Fort Chadbourne in Runnels County, about two hundred and forty miles west of Mexia. Once back on the ranch, he asked Mr. Spillar if he could have three or four weeks off before he went back to work. Mr. Spillar gave Jim the extra time, no questions asked. Jim had been a strong worker at his ranch and had fought for their town and the Confederacy. It was the least he could do for a man who had done so much for him and the people of Mexia. He asked the Pruitts, too, if they minded watching Little Ruth for a while longer. They were happy to oblige as having Little Ruth in their home helped keep their mind off losing

Laurie. He didn't tell them he was thinking of moving away. It was just too difficult for him to continue in Mexia, where everything he saw reminded him of Laurie and the life they shared together.

Bright and early the next Monday morning, Jim headed west toward Runnels county. It was a bright, cloudless day – a day that makes you glad you are alive. It was a day, he thought, like so many he had spent with Laurie. He was riding Charlie for the first time in a long while. While doing his ranch work, he mostly used the Spillar horses in his string. Charlie was, for all intents and purposes, semi-retired.

The trees were just beginning to bud with the first flush of springtime. Texas was a beautiful state, especially this time of year. The animals had not had enough exposure to humans to be afraid and played joyfully around Jim as he rode west.

The first large settlement he encountered was Waco, which had the Brazos river running through its city limits. Waco had been the starting place of the 10th Texas Infantry, Jim's old military unit.

Jim stopped at the general store and asked if anyone knew Colonel Nelson. An older lady behind the counter said she did but didn't know if he was back from the war. Someone standing nearby said Nelson and a few of his troops found General Forrest near Selma, Alabama and fought with him. Jim explained to the people in the store that Colonel Nelson had released them in Nashville and told them to go home. Though he knew the war was lost,

Jim said, Colonel Nelson felt honor-bound to fight until the formal surrender.

A man stepped forward and said that Colonel Nelson had a place where his wife and children lived on the outskirts of the settlement and that he should go by and see them. He explained to Jim that news was scarce with almost no mail delivery due to Reconstruction. Following the directions the man gave him, Jim eventually came upon the commander's home. It was a simple but impressive dwelling with everything in its rightful place.

Jim tied Charlie to the hitching post and climbed the steps leading to the front door. He knocked and a petite and distinguished looking lady opened the door.

"I'm Mrs. Nelson," she said sweetly. "May I help you?"

"I'm Jim Walker and I served in your husband's unit in Tennessee," Jim explained. "I have not seen or heard from your husband since the Battle of Nashville. I wanted to express my thanks for your husband's contribution to the war effort and make sure if you and your children are alright."

Mrs. Nelson seemed legitimately stunned to see someone from her husband's unit. She quickly asked him to come into the house and offered him a cup of coffee.

"Coffee would be good, ma'am," Jim said, "if it's not too much a bother."

"Not at all," she said graciously. "It's such a joy to meet someone who served with my husband."

"I haven't seen him since he released my unit at Nashville," Jim explained. At that time, he was in excellent physical condition and still dedicated to the cause."

"I haven't received any specific information since the end of the war," she told Jim. "This was some time after Lee surrendered at Appomattox and that was two years ago. Some of his colleagues contacted me to tell me he'd been captured while attempting to smuggle Jefferson Davis, the Confederate president, out of the country to freedom. I don't know exactly where he is in prison, but I've been told he's in good health and will be released soon. Dedication has a price and my husband is paying his share."

She sat back and looked at Jim carefully.

"Are you still dedicated to the cause?" She asked carefully.

"Well, honestly, I haven't thought we could win the war since the summer of '63 after our losses at Gettysburg and Vicksburg," Jim answered thoughtfully. "I believe the battles at Franklin and Nashville were pointless and only served to put our men in harm's way. A lot of blood was spilled and a lot of commendable young men were killed. I think it's time to turn our weapons into plow shares and cease killing on the battlefield."

Jim stopped and bowed his head slightly.

"I'm sorry, ma'am," he said, "sometimes I get carried away with the senselessness of war. I know Colonel Nelson feels the same way, but he will not vent his true feelings in front of his subordinates. I'm afraid too many of our leaders from both sides have learned to love it too much. Your husband is not one of these men. He is merely caught up in the whirlwind of war. I know he feels an overwhelming responsibility to his oath and his man. He is a legitimate hero who puts his men and responsibilities first. Otherwise, he would be home with you and his family."

Jim felt his eyes begin to fill with tears, just a bit at first, and then he broke down and wept openly. Mrs. Nelson sat down with a handkerchief, in which she buried her face and let her emotions out. Though he felt a bit uncomfortable, as this was Colonel Nelson's wife, he wanted to hold her and reassure her that everything would be alright.

Just then a boy ran into the room.

"What's wrong, Mama?" He asked, his face flushed. "Has something happened to Daddy?"

"Oh no, son," Mrs. Nelson, replied in a comforting tone. "This is Mr. Walker who signed up as a lieutenant in your Daddy's regiment. He just came by to pay his respects and see if there was any news about your father. I just couldn't help myself from crying. It was too much to hold in anymore. I'm sorry for my outburst."

"A good cry heals the soul," Jim told her. "If anyone has the right to cry, you do."

"Thank you, Mr. Walker. I appreciate your encouragement," she said, turning then to her son. "I'd like to introduce you to my son, Wayne, who is fourteen years of age. We also have a daughter named Dorothy who is ten. They haven't seen their Father since the fall of '64. They miss him so."

Mrs. Nelson asked Jim to have lunch with them and the children thought it was a wonderful idea. He was concerned about the imposition of her cooking and the possible lack of food since the war had exhausted everything. He accepted her invitation, though, and enjoyed spending time with a real family again. He felt comfortable with Mrs. Nelson and her children. He felt as though he'd know them all his life.

Mrs. Nelson asked if he was married and he told her about Laurie and his two children. When he said that he had lost his son and Laurie during the epidemic, Mrs. Nelson began to weep again.

Jim told her it was still very sad and hard for him to think about his loss. He said that he'd been told it would get easier with time, but it hadn't yet. That was the reason he was going to Runnels county, he explained, because everything in Mexia reminded him of his family.

Mrs. Nelson mentioned he should check with the local sheriff to make sure the passage to Runnels was clear. There had been some real problems with Indians between Hamilton and Brownwood. The Indians knew the armies of both the North and South were fighting each other and had very little time to devote to protecting their villages. They consequently felt more at liberty to conduct raids of all sorts.

After lunch, Jim told her he had to go and planned to talk to the local sheriff. As he left, he gave Mrs. Nelson and her children a hug and told them Colonel Nelson was lucky to have such a wonderful family.

29

TRIP TO RUNNELS COUNTY

Jim left the Nelson home with a tear running down his cheek. He walked out and dug in saddlebags to find an apple to give to Charlie. As she took the apple, she brought her head up and down with her mane flowing in the breeze. It was her way of showing her appreciation to her friend. Jim then tightened his cinch strap, mounted Charlie, and rode off in search of the sheriff's office.

When Jim reached the sheriff's office, he wrapped Charlie's reins on a hitching post and went into the sheriff's office. Inside, he saw a large man sitting with his boots crossed on top of his desk.

"Howdy, stranger! I'm John Young, the sheriff of McLennan county," John said with a smile on his face, "and who are you?"

John Young was what most imagine to be a stereotypical western sheriff. His face was rugged with a large handlebar mustache, green eyes, and a ruddy complexion. Even sitting down, he had his gun belt on with a .44 caliber revolver tied low on his hip. Jim could tell just by looking at him that he was not someone to be trifled with.

"Good afternoon, sheriff," Jim began. "My name is Jim Walker. I served with Colonel Nelson during the war. I'm heading for Runnels county and stopped here to check in on the colonel's family. Mrs. Nelson said that I should check with you before heading to Runnels to see if the Indians might be on the prowl."

"Yessir," Sheriff Young replied. "The Indians have been killing and raiding. They come down from Llano Estacado raiding and leaving before we can do anything about it. We have some Rangers, but not enough to be effective. My deputies consist of old men and young boys who are not of fighting age. You know that means they're young because 14-year-old boys have died in this war. It's a terrible thing."

The sheriff looked down and then back at Jim.

"You should be safe until you pass Brownwood, but there is a lot of Indian activity past there as you approach Runnels county and the settlement of Ballinger. It is my understanding that when the Indians got too out of hand, the citizens moved into the deserted Fort Phantom Hill. That is a fort that was abandoned by the Yankees at the start of the War of Northern aggression. The Confederates took possession of it, but didn't have enough men or arms to establish it as a permanent garrison."

The sheriff took a deep breath.

"Contingents of Russian immigrants have settled in Runnels county and there has been a battle between the Indians and them since then. The Russians are attempting to raise wheat as a cash crop, but the Indians come in and steal their livestock and burn their crops. Here lately, the immigrants spend more time in the fort than they do working their fields, but they refuse to give up."

"Well, sheriff," Jim asked, "what do you suggest?"

"Well, I would suggest settling somewhere else," the sheriff responded flatly, "but if your mind is made up, I would be careful going through Brownwood and only travel at night on your way to Ballinger. Have you ever had to fight Indians?"

"Oh, yes," Jim replied. "I've had to fight more than I wanted to. Due to my time in the war and protecting the citizens in Mexia from Indian attacks, I've done enough fighting to last ten lifetimes. Now I know why the land in Runnels county is so inexpensive. I'll leave here at about 4:00 this afternoon and travel all night. I'm not looking forward to making this journey, but if it was easy, I probably couldn't afford the land."

Jim thanks Sheriff Young and then dropped by the general store to thank the lady who had directed him to Colonel Nelson's home. The lady asked Jim if he found the home and if everything was alright. He replied it was and was grateful for her help.

While there, Jim also bought four boxes of ammunition for his Henry repeating rifle and five boxes for his two forty-four six shooters. He knew that one man with that much firepower could hold off hostiles for a long time.

Before leaving, he got a couple bars of stick candy and a cold soda pop. He thanked the lady and mounted Charlie to head west.

Once on his journey, he discovered that the roads west were not really roads, but paths made by mounted men and a few wagons and carriages. According to the lady at the store, Wells Fargo had planned a route in this part of Texas, but had to cancel their plans due to the war.

The other travelers on the path who were also just passing through. Following their guidance, Jim did not ride directly on what passed as a road, knowing that was where an attack could occur.

After Waco, the next settlement he would come across was Hamilton. He figured he would reach it by daylight the following day. When there, he planned to visit the local law enforcement agency and make them aware of who he was and his business in their town. He would gather as much information from them as possible, especially regarding the probability of encountering any Indians or Comancheros. He then planned to find a shade tree and bed down until it was almost dark. By then, he would be due some rest.

30

HOMESTEADER ATTACK

As was the case so many times in Mexia, a Comanche moon once hung above Jim in the Texas skies. It was so bright, it was almost daylight. The Indians took advantage of the light of this sort of moon to go on their raids, which is how it earned its name. In a way, Jim liked it as he could see, but he knew the dangers it could bring, too. During his night travels, he passed many forted-up ranch houses. The windows were enclosed by heavy wooden shutters with gun ports. Jim guessed the shutters were locked from the interior.

On the ranches, the people had their livestock shut up in barns that could be seen from their houses. Each house had at least two dogs to alert them with barking should any unwelcome guests come calling.

When it was almost midnight, Jim saw some movement ahead and pulled up under shadows cast by a tall cottonwood tree. From this spot, he could see about six Indians attempting to steal the horses from a corral near a farmhouse just ahead. It looked like the dogs had been killed by arrows so the people in the house were unaware of what was happening so near their home.

As the Indians moved silently in a group toward the pen of horses, Jim pulled his rifle out of his saddle's scabbard and jumped down on the ground. He took a bead on the lead Indian and fired. He fired quickly and accurately, then hitting the three men in front. The uninjured Indians fled toward their horses but were cut down by Jim before they could mount and ride away.

The farmers in the home were unsure of what was happening outside their home. They opened the wooden shutters to see Jim examining the fallen Indians.

"What's going on out there?" A voice from the interior finally called.

"My name is Jim Walker," Jim shouted toward the caller, "and I was just riding by when I saw these Indians trying to steal your horses."

The front door opened. The light from a kerosene lamp illuminated the cabin just enough for Jim to see a man, a woman, and two small children inside.

The man walked briskly toward Jim.

"My name is Fritz Bauer," the man said trying to catch his breath. "That's my wife Hannah and two children in the doorway. We are so grateful for your help. We've been out here only two years with only minor trouble from Indians so far."

"I hope this doesn't cause you any trouble with retaliation," Jim said. "I think we should take the bodies away from here and bury them. That way any other Indians will not know what happened."

It was still night, but the light from the moon allowed them to go about their task fairly easily. Fritz harnessed his team to a wagon and helped Jim load the slain Indians in the back along with some picks and shovels.

Jim and Fritz climbed into the wagon and drove roughly four miles into the midst of a grove of trees. It took almost until sunrise before they were able to finish digging a hole big and deep enough to bury the dead Indians.

The loose dirt remaining after the hole was covered was shoveled into the wagon and the fresh grave was covered with leaves. It would be very difficult to see that anyone had been buried there. At least that's what Jim and Fritz hoped. On the way back to Adrian's homestead, the loose dirt was shoveled out of the wagon a little at a time.

When they got back to the house, Mrs. Bauer had breakfast ready. They had just killed a hog and had plenty of fresh bacon and ham. It seems the horrific events of the last few hours would stifle one's appetite, but after everything Jim had been through in the past few years, it seemed he was numb to death.

Over breakfast, Jim explained to the Bauers where he was going and why he was riding past at night when he saw the Indians stealing their horses. Mrs. Bauer told him that he was welcome to sleep at their house until night fell again. Mr. Bauer agreed and told Jim it was the least they could do to show their appreciation.

That evening, Mrs. Bauer, or Hannah, as she preferred to be called, fixed a supper for Jim that consisted of pinto beans, potatoes, corn, hominy grits, and thick-crusted apple pie. He ate so much he was afraid he'd have trouble mounting Charlie.

After the meal, Jim and the Bauers had some time to visit. Fritz told Jim they had immigrated into Texas in the 1850's with a large contingence of Germans from Indianola on the Texas Gulf Coast. They first settled in the Texas Hill Country around Fredericksburg. They had, however, been lured to their current property by the promise of cheap land.

As Jim prepared to leave, he jokingly told the Bauers he would stop by on his way back to taste some more of Hannah's apple pie. The sun had just settled in the western sky when he swung into the saddle and headed toward Runnels County.

31

MEETING WITH TEXAS RANGERS

Charlie broke into an easy trot and kept that pace for a couple of hours. Eventually, she came upon a stream where Jim walked Charley out into the water and let her have a drink. Not far away, Jim heard voices and water splashing. The voices were speaking English. As carefully as he could, he called out to the distant voices. The voices hushed for a moment but soon a group of men came down to where Jim was half-hidden behind a large cottonwood tree.

The man in a front, wearing a large-brimmed hat, introduced himself as J.B. Walters. He told Jim that he and his friend were Texas Rangers stationed in Austin, who were scouting through Indian country. Jim explained who he was and told them about his experience at the Bauer homestead. J.B. said he could use a good man like Jim in the Rangers.

"I'm on my way to Runnels county to buy some land for a possible homestead," Jim told him.

"We're headed over to Ballinger," J.B. replied, "Why don't you ride along with us for protection and get to know the boys?"

Since Ballinger was the county seat of Runnels, Jim agreed. He reined Charlie to group in with the rest of the Rangers and headed out with them.

They were not far from Hamilton when J.B. told Jim there was a safehouse there that consisted of two rooms: a kitchen and a long room used for sleeping quarters. Since he and the Rangers had been riding for almost two days straight, he had his group planned to sleep for a bit before heading on to Ballinger. Buck Jackson, one of the Rangers, asked if they wanted him to rustle up some food, but J.B. told him he'd rather sleep a few hours first if it was all the same to him. At the house, two men stood guard duty for two hours at a time and would then switch out with another two men so that everyone got a chance to rest.

Jim woke to the smell of coffee and frying bacon. When he looked around, he saw that he was the only one still in bed. He quickly went out back to a cluster of oak trees and relieved himself. As he came back into the house, J.B. was standing there smiling.

"There's an outhouse with paper on the west side of the house," he told Jim.

"I didn't know and I was in somewhat of a hurry," Jim replied sheepishly.

The men had a laugh and told him to grab a plate and dig in. His breakfast was getting cold.

After breakfast, Jim and the men took care of their horses and equipment. On a scout, they never took off their saddles – they simply loosened the cinches and removed the bits of the bridles from the horse's mouth. Each horse was hobbled to allow for grazing, but otherwise had limited movement. Jim had a sack of oats hung over the back of his saddle with sugar sticks tucked away in his saddle bags.

J.B. organized his men into a squad formation and called roll. Not surprisingly, everyone was present and accounted for. After mounting their horses, everyone headed west with J.B. and Jim in the lead.

The ride to Ballinger was uneventful except for a couple of homesteaders who had been attacked and lost their horses and some other livestock. The Indians didn't like cattle because they ate too much grass intended for the buffalo. Horses, on the other hand, were extremely valuable to them. On their raids, they would usually run cattle out into an open pasture, kill them, take some choice cuts, and let the buzzards feast on the carcasses of the rotting flesh that was left.

As the men arrived in Ballinger, Jim asked J.B. how long he thought they would be in town.

"Probably a couple of days within the immediate vicinity," J.B. answered. "We need to check with local law enforcement agencies to look into what's happening at Fort Phantom Hill. It shouldn't take over two days. That should give you some time to think over becoming a Ranger and check on the possibility of obtaining some farmland. We'll meet you in front of the courthouse at around six in the evening exactly two days from today."

After saying goodbye to J.B. and the men, Jim noticed a large sign that read "Hays Land Company". He didn't know if they sold land, but if they didn't, they probably knew who was in that business.

"Let's go look into buying some land," Jim said, nudging Charlie before dismounting her. "I'll be back in a little while."

32

JIM BECOMES LANDOWNER

Jim walked into the office where a young lady stood behind the counter. She asked Jim if she could be of service to him. He replied that he hoped so and told her he was looking for some farm and grazing land. He also explained that he was a veteran of the war and was looking for some affordable land to settle and work.

The girl was about twenty years of age and stood approximately five feet tall. She had blonde curls that dropped almost to her waist and had a look of effortless sophistication coupled with simplicity. This was not uncommon of girls who possessed good breeding and had been reared on the Texas frontier.

"My name is Kim Burton," she said. "I just work in the office as a clerk, but I can show you some maps with the acreage pinpointed and give you the approximate costs per acre. Mr. Paskel is the broker and has the power to finalize any deals. Are you looking for a home to settle or just ranchland to run a herd?"

Jim explained that he had lost his young wife and child in Mexia and just wanted a fresh start somewhere. Kim expressed her condolences and said they would be happy to have him as a new resident.

"When does Mr. Paskel get back to the office?" Jim asked.

"That's him tying up to the hitching rail now," Kim replied, looking out the window. Let me introduce the two of you and get you each a cup of coffee."

A tall, lean man probably in his mid-forties came into the front door. He said hello to Kim and then directed his attention to Jim. Mr. Paskel was over six feet in height and had lightly graying hair and a handlebar moustache. He looked more like someone who would be singing tenor in a barbershop quartet than selling land in a territory rife with Indian activity.

"My name is Tom Paskel and I'm the broker here. Let me put my coat and bags in the office and I'll be right with you. I'm sorry, I didn't catch your name?"

"I'm Jim Walker from Mexia," Jim said. "How much is good land selling for in Runnels County these days?"

"Good land is running about $10 an acre for up to two-hundred acres and as you go up in size, the price decreases," Mr. Paskel answered. "This includes mineral, surface, and subsurface water rights. Most dug wells are roughly fifteen to twenty feet deep. We also have a running stream that runs year-round which is a real asset, especially when running grazing livestock. How much are you looking to buy, Mr. Walker?"

"Let's look at properties between one and two hundred acres and you can tell me about the Indian problems," Jim replied.

"We do have a problem with Indians, but we're hoping that will be remedied with the fort being re-established," Mr. Paskel said. "Why do you think land is so cheap? The value of the land is directly connected to the Indian problems."

Jim and Mr. Paskel spent the next two days looking at land all over the county with Jim deciding on a two-hundred-acre tract with a fine creek running through it with a fine creek running through it and laced with cottonwood trees. He made his decision to buy while sitting on the shaded bank watching the birds and squirrels playing in the branches of the large trees.

"Jim," Mr. Paskel said, "You are one of the few Anglos buying land here. My biggest customers have been a few Mexicans and a large contingent of Russians. The Russians have bought a lot of land and are raising wheat. They seem to be a vigorous and hearty bunch. The fierce bands of Indians do not seem to be a problem to them. Even if they lost someone, they would be back in the fields the next morning at sunup as though nothing had happened. Within another three months, we are hoping the Indian problem will be solved."

"I hope so, too," Jim replied. "I expect to move here and raise a family."

"There is a colonel named Randall McKenzie, who is a commander of Fort Richardson at Jacksboro," Mr. Paskel said, "who I've heard just defeated Quanah Parker at a battle in Palo Duro canyon. He killed their mounts and made them walk all the way back to their reservation at Fort Sill."

This was like what happened to the Indians' horses back at Mexia, thought Tom.

Back at the land office, Jim and Mr. Paskel made out a contract with $500 down and the rest financed by Mr. Paskel on a ten-year term mortgage at 10% interest. The deed was executed and filed in the Runnels County Clerk's office in Ballinger. Jim was a landowner and a happy one. He just wished Laurie was there to share his excitement. Having accomplished his mission, Jim set out that night for Mexia.

On the way home, Jim again rode mostly at night. He thought about stopping by to see the Bauers, but he had so much to do and little time to do it. He was going to go by and speak with Mr. Spillar about starting a herd of about twenty-five heifers and two bulls. He was willing to give Mr. Spillar the first calving crop and half the profits on his first sale of cattle the coming year.

Jim had a pretty good nest egg from the sale of the place where he and Laurie had lived in Mexia. He had also gotten all his back pay when he mustered out of the army. Of course, this was all Confederate money, but he had converted it into land and other tangible goods before it became completely worthless.

He had to use this money to buy a team of horses with a wagon and a turning plow while leaving enough cash to build some type of living quarters in the beginning. He was excited and hopeful that Mr. Spillar would be agreeable to his deal.

He rode into Mexia three days later without encountering any problems at all. He was tired, but he was more excited than sleepy. He wanted to ride by the Pruitts and see Little Ruth and his in-laws again. He still wasn't sure what he was going to do with Little Ruth, but he knew present-day Runnels County was no place for a little girl with no mommy. Nevertheless, he wanted Little Ruth to remember him as a loving daddy and not someone who came to visit from time to time.

When he went by the Pruitts, he spoke to them about his little girl and they said they were more than happy to keep his baby until he got on his feet. They said they hated to see him take Little Ruth so far away but understood the difficulty of the painful reminders Mexia held for him. He didn't tell them about the proposition to Mr. Spillar about starting the herd. He wanted to make sure Mr. Spillar agreed before mentioning it to anyone. That night, he ate supper with the Pruitts and reminisced about happier times. The memories brought tears to everyone's eyes and gave the evening a heartbreaking ambience. Jim finally broke the sad mood by walking to each of the Pruitts and giving them a hug.

After Jim left, Mrs. Pruitt told her husband that it was unusual for Jim to give him a hug, but said it was a sign of his sensitivity and sweetness.

It was roughly seven o'clock when Jim arrived on the Spillar Ranch. The sun was just beginning to hide behind the trees to the rear of the ranch house. He tied Charlie to the hitching rail and walked up the porch and knocked on the door. The youngest of the Spillar girls answered.

"It's Jim! It's Jim!" She squealed with excitement upon seeing him. "Everybody come see! Jim's back!"

The little girl threw herself into him and hugged him tight around the waist. It wasn't long before Mr. and Mrs. Spillar and the rest of the children were running into the room.

"We're so happy to see you and know that you're alright," Mr. Pruitt said with a big smile on his face. "We've already eaten, but there's plenty and I'm sure we can find you something."

"No, thank you," Jim said, just as happy to see the Spillar family. "I dropped by to see Little Ruth and ate with the Pruitts, but I appreciate your kind offer."

Mr. Spillar fixed some coffee and he and his wife and Jim retired into the family room. They were anxious to learn as much as possible about Jim's adventures in Runnels County. Jim told them he had purchased two hundred acres with the opportunity to purchase more when he could.

"I know you're aware of this," Jim said, "but it's the little things you don't really think about that really add up in expenses."

Mr. Spillar said he understand and, without meaning to pry, asked Jim if he was having money problems.

"Not really," Jim replied, "but I'm trying to start a herd and that's a big investment. I've got good water and grazing land and thought I would put about fifty acres into it for some sort of feed crop for the cattle I don't have. I want to offer a business proposal to you where I would take twenty-five heifers and two bulls with the understanding that the first calving crop would be yours along with fifty percent of the profit on the sale of any cattle for the first two years."

"Jim," Mr. Spillar said, a bit taken aback, "that is too much. We consider you part of the family. You have done a great deal for the ranch and have acted so honorably as a soldier for our country. I want to offer you twenty-five head of bred heifers and two bulls to start your ranch. I'll also throw in a good wagon, four plow horses, and a few tools to include a turning plow, posthole diggers, and anything within reason you need to start from scratch."

"I can't let you do this," Jim said, shocked. "That's a lot of money."

"You've earned a lot more than what we are offering you, Jim," Mr. Spillar replied. "I just wish we could do more. You're a good man, Jim Jefferson Walker, and it is our pleasure to assist you in any way. We need more men like you in Texas to help re-build the state after the dreadful war we've just been through."

Jim couldn't wrap his head around Mr. Spillars kindness, but Mr. Spillar wasn't done.

"You will need drovers to herd your livestock, drive your wagon, and a team of horses. They will all be necessary to get the cattle drive to your new homestead in Runnels County."

"I really don't know what to say," Jim said gratefully, "except thank you and I'll pay you back when I can."

After this talk with Mr. Spillar, Jim was well on his way to achieving his new dream. God was good.

33

JIM MEETS NEW WIFE

Jim spent the night in the bunkhouse and got up early. After drinking a cup of coffee, he saddled Charlie and headed into town. His first stop was the hardware store where he purchased items such as staples and fence wire.

The young lady behind the counter introduced herself as Amanda Hughes. She said her father owned the store and she had just started working there as a full-time employee a month earlier. Jim told her he had lived in Mexia off and on for several years, but he didn't think he recognized her.

"I've been back east for over five years at Mary Baldwin College in Staunton, Virginia," she explained. "My parents sent me off to college and the war broke out. I was afraid to cross the country during the fight, so after I finished my bachelor's degree, I went on to get a master's degree in liberal arts. When the war was over, I came home. I missed Mexia and the people here."

Jim was impressed with the educated woman who stood before him.

"What about you?" She asked. "I don't remember you when I was growing up here as a child."

Jim took the next few minutes to bring her up to date on his history and what he was attempting to do in Runnels county. He couldn't help but be a bit smitten with her as she was unlike anyone he'd ever met. He knew, though, that a woman with such sophistication could do much better than someone like him. The conversation between them went well, but he was sure she agreed that he was not in her league.

After making his purchases and loading the wagon, Amanda locked eyes with him and asked how long he was going to be in town. He told her he wasn't sure, but he had to purchase a wagon and team, farm implements, and whatever he would need to start his ranch near Ballinger.

"Good," she replied. "That will give you time to take me to lunch at the new buffet that just opened and the dance on Friday night. "Am I too forward? Maybe so, but I've become older after being introduced to more liberal ideas in college. I've learned that if you want something in life, you should simply go for it. What do you think?"

"Yes, that would be nice," Jim answered, stuttering. "Do I get to pick the day or do you pick that, too?"

"Today would be nice as we never know what tomorrow will bring," Amanda answered. "We can walk to the luncheonette from here and get to know each other better on the way."

Jim said he would come back at around eleven o'clock to beat the lunchtime rush. She agreed and said she would see him then.

Jim felt excited. He couldn't believe that another wonderful woman had shown interest in him after Laurie. He knew that he would always love Laurie and no one would ever take her place in his heart, but he also knew that he had to move on and spending time with Miss Amanda Hughes was a step in the right direction.

He rode Charlie over the wagon yard and purchased a good, solid used wagon and then considered his need for four good draft horses to pull a wagon and plow. He would also need a full complement of leather harnesses. He rode over to the ranch to see if Mr. Spillar had any ideas who and where to get the horses and the harnesses. Mr. Spillar was somewhat taken aback at the idea of Jim buying a wagon when he had several he could give him.

"Jim," Mr. Spillar said, "go and see if you can get your money back and I'll outfit you with a good constellation wagon, a team of four draft horses, a harness, some plows, and everything you need to get started."

"You have already been so unbelievably good to me," Jim said, shocked. "I can't take any more!"

"You can and you will," Mr. Spillar replied. "You can pay me back quicker if you have the means to get started. I'm doing it because I want to but also because I'm a little selfish regarding the return of my investment. Now let's go pick four good draft horses, harnesses, a wagon, and whatever else you might need to start the Walker Ranch."

First, Jim went back to the wagon yard to see if he could get his money back on the wagon he'd just purchased. The owner agreed as wagons were in short supply and he knew it would sell again quickly. No money had changed hands, so the cancellation was a simple matter.

This took a load off Jim's mind. After taking care of the wagon business, he headed over to the hardware store to pick up Amanda for their lunch engagement. Luckily, the hardware store was close as Jim had no transportation except for Amanda riding behind him on Charlie.

She probably would have no reservations about doing that, Jim thought to himself. *She is a real woman who doesn't seem to be concerned about doing what others might consider unladylike.*

Jim smiled to himself as he guided Charlie up to the hitching rail in front of the hardware store.

Amanda was standing in front of the store with a wide smile on her face.

"It's about time, Jim Walker," she said laughing. "I've had several offers for a luncheon date in the past few minutes."

"Were they as handsome and wealthy as I am?" Jim quipped.

"Of course not," Amanda said, not missing a beat. "That's why I'm still standing here. Are you ready to dine with the Queen of Limestone County?"

"Absolutely, your highness," Jim replied, bowing. "Would you like to ride behind me on my noble steed or walk beside me to the royal dining hall?"

"It wouldn't be the first time I've ridden double on a horse," she said, "but I feel more like walking today. I'd also like to introduce you to my father, Jack Hughes."

As they entered the store together, Amanda began to walk toward an older man at the back of the store.

"Dad, I'd like to introduce you to someone," Amanda said assuredly.

Amanda's father looked up, waved his hand, and came to meet them.

"Dad, this is Jim Walker," she started, "he has been affiliated with Mr. Spillar of Mexia for roughly ten years as a ranch hand and foreman. He was also a lieutenant in the 10th Texas Regiment during the late war."

"I've heard of you, Jim," Mr. Hughes said, extending his hand. "Word has spread about your involvement in ending the great Indian raids in and around Mexia. I've known the Pruitts for a long time, too. I heard you married Laurie and just lost her and a child not long ago. I'm sorry for your loss. I know the whole town was overwhelmed with grief when that epidemic spread."

Jim looked down at the floor and Mr. Hughes immediately apologized for mentioning such sad occurrences.

"It's alright." Jim said quickly, "I think about it all the time, but I think she would like for me to go on."

"Dad, I'm going to lunch with Jim," Amanda said. "I'll be back in about an hour or so. Do you think you can handle the fort while I'm gone?"

She smiled at her father, her eyes twinkling.

"I think I'll manage somehow," Mr. Hughes replied, laughing. "You two have a good time. Jim, it was nice to formally meet you. You should be warned that my girl is pretty headstrong. She takes after her mother, but we've been married for thirty years, so it's worked out well for us."

"See you later, Dad," Amanda said as they strolled out the door toward the cafeteria.

The special on the menu that day at the cafeteria was pretty much the same as every other day: chicken fried steak, hash browns, gravy, salad, and hot rolls. Jim was hungry, but his mind was on the lovely Amanda, who had bewitched him with her confidence and beauty.

Once they settled down to eat, Amanda did not mince words.

"What's the plan for the rest of your life?" She asked Jim pointedly.

"Well, I plan to build the Walker Ranch in Runnels county and make it the biggest and best ranch in all of Texas," Jim replied excitedly.

Then, with a sudden burst of gusto, he turned the tables on her.

"And what are your plans for the rest of *your* life, Amanda?"

"Well, first, I'd like to be the wife of the man who builds the biggest and best ranch in Texas," she replied without taking a breath. "Furthermore, I'd like the ranch to be called the JWA Ranch for the Jim Walker Ranch...and the 'A' standing for Amanda. Time is short and decisions have to be made or lost forever. I've taken a quick liking to you and I think it'd be a short distance to loving you. I feel friendship is more important than what most people call love...at least in the beginning."

Jim sat at the table across from her, his mouth agape with a half-eaten piece of steak still in it.

"Is this a proposal of marriage?" He asked, completely shocked.

"I think it would be, in the beginning, a partnership consisting of respect and friendship with love growing over time," Amanda replied.

Jim settled back in his chair, his mind reeling. How could this woman make something so bold and unexpected actually make good sense?

"Oh, Jim," she went on. "I know you! Everyone in this town knows you and they all love you, including my folks. I don't really feel comfortable being so forthright, but this is something I want and I know I could make you a good wife and companion."

"I feel honored," Jim said, blushing. "I think you'd be an ideal wife to helping in building a ranch. "When will you be ready to go or would you rather wait until I have established a little organization in the place?"

"No," she replied shaking her head. "I want to be a partner from the get-go, but we need to get married for things to look proper.

"We also have to take my daughter, Little Ruth, into consideration," he told her. "I'm not sure it would be prudent to take her until a shelter is built. She is currently with her grandparents and they love her so much."

"We'll have to tell my parents, the Pruitts, and the Spillar family," Amanda added.

The rest of the week went by in a blur with getting the wagon and filling it with all the necessary supplies. They picked out heifers and bulls, selected drivers, and began to head west on Saturday morning. It was an exciting time for

Jim and Amanda, who were married the next Friday night in a simple ceremony with only the Hughes, Pruitts, Spillars, and a few close friends present. Such a short time ago, Jim had absolutely no idea that when he returned to Runnels county he would have a wife and all of the necessary goods to start a new ranch and new life. Everyone, including Jim, felt it was prudent to leave Little Ruth with the Pruitts until they got settled into their new home.

34

THE TRIP TO BALLINGER

At the Spillar Ranch, they were ready to start with the cattle penned in the corral and the wagon filled to the brim with their new supplies. As they were getting ready to leave, eight cowpokes who were also part-time Rangers, rode up with Mr. Spillar.

"I'm taking a little more precaution than I originally thought necessary," Mr. Spillar told Jim. "Those beeves and draft horses would make an inviting target for marauding Indians and I want to protect my investments and loved ones."

Jim shook Mr. Spillar's hand and Mr. Spillar pulled him into a bear hug, telling him how special he was to his family and himself. He then hugged Amanda and told her to take care of Jim and Little Ruth when she joined them at the new ranch. The Spillars had known Amanda all her life except for the five years she spent in Virginia. With tears in their eyes, the group said their goodbyes and Jim slapped the reins on the horse's rump and they were off to Runnels county.

As they began their ride, Jim asked the Rangers what kind of formation would be best. How many drovers vs. outriders would provide them the optimum amount of protection?

One of the Rangers spoke up and told Jim that he thought five drovers could manage the herd with three outriders. They assigned one outrider to the extreme right, one to the extreme left, and one to the front with the formation resembling a wedge. If any one of the outriders saw anything suspicious, they would ride hard for the main party, which included the wagon and cattle. If there was imminent danger, the outrider who spotted it would fire his six shooter, making everyone aware that a dangerous situation was about to happen.

Jim was familiar with this sort of tactic as he had used it in the army and while with the Rangers. The group had decided that Jim would be in overall command while Amanda acted as wagon boss and fed the troops while maintain an inventory of the water and firewood. The men themselves would share the duties of collecting things like water and firewood so no one person would have to do it all. Jim was confident in the men that accompanied men, as he had never known a Ranger to shirk his duties. Jim assessed they would arrive in Ballinger in four or five days, "Lord willing and the creek don't rise."

The first day was uneventful, with no one sighting anything hostile other than a couple of rattlesnakes. It was a bright spring day with the sun shining and flowers blooming. It was one of those days that made you feel glad you're alive. The first night they encamped on the banks of a running creek which provided water for the livestock and to wash the cooking utensils. The drovers made plans regarding the number of night riders and their rotation to guard and protect the herd.

Amanda handled the position of wagon boss very well. She cooked supper and washed the utensils with help from Jim. By seven o'clock, everyone had their bedrolls laid out and the night riders were in place guarding the cattle. Everyone had a good, restful sleep that night that energized them for the ride ahead the next day.

The next morning, Amanda woke early and started the fire for coffee and breakfast. The men were used to getting up early with coffee as it was their best prop to sustain them on long working days. Black coffee opened their eyes and kept them going for as long as they needed.

After breakfast, the men made sure their horses were fed and watered, un-hobbled, and saddled for the day's work. By six o'clock, it was "Westward, ho!"

Jim and Amanda figured they would reach Waco and the Brazos river on the second day. The river could be a formidable obstacle for the cattle to cross. They didn't know if the river was low enough or how many would fit on the ferry if they had to take that route.

They would just have to wait and see.

35

CROSSING THE BRAZOS AT WACO

At about four o'clock in the afternoon, the city of Waco came into view. Jim rode out to the Rangers driving the cattle and asked their advice on crossing. He knew they had been here many more times than he had on their Ranger scouts.

A Ranger named Emmitt Bailey stepped forward and said there was a really good spot for crossing up ahead. Emmitt told Jim the easy crossing was the primary reason the town was built there.

"OK," Jim replied. "We'll camp here for the night and cross at first light in the morning. Let's take the horses down to the river and let them drink, get some grub, and get ready to cross the river at first light. We've still got a long way to go."

The next morning, they discovered that not only was the river low enough to cross but also the wagon. This good fortune not only saved them money, but also a vast amount of time. They had traveled roughly eighty miles with no mishaps. They felt lucky to have had such easy route so far.

They left the bank of the Brazos at Waco for their next stop at Valley Mills, followed by a stop at Hamilton before reaching Ballinger in Runnels county. Their best estimate for arrival was four more days assuming no major problems.

Jim told Amanda about the run-in with the Indians at the Bauer homestead between Hamilton and Ballinger. He told her he wanted to stop by and see if they were alright. Everyone was concerned about the Indians discovering their slain comrades in the shallow grave that had been dug that night. Jim was concerned about the Indians tracing everything back to the Bauer's land where it had happened.

"That's good that you're concerned, Jim," Amanda said. "I'd like to meet the Bauers, too."

"I'm not absolutely sure exactly where it was when I came onto the property during the night, but I think I would recognize it," Jim told her.

He was right. When they came out of Hamilton after a full day's travel, when Jim raised his hand over his head.

"Wait a minute," he said. "I think this is it. This is the Bauer homestead."

After pulling in front of the main house, Jim and Amanda went to the front door and knocked.

"Who is it?" A voice called from inside.

"It's Jim Walker," Jim replied. "I was the one who helped with your Indian raid not long ago."

"Oh, Jim!" Mrs. Bauer said, swinging the door open. "It's so good to see you again. Come in. My husband is out checking the livestock as the Indians have been more active lately."

Jim stepped forward and motioned to Amanda.

"Mrs. Bauer," Jim said with a smile, "I'd like to introduce you to my new wife, Amanda."

"Oh! I didn't know you were married, Jim," Mrs. Bauer replied.

"He wasn't until last Friday night," Amanda laughed.

"Well, congratulations, Amanda! You've got a good man!" Mrs. Bauer said, smiling. "He sure saved our bacon when we came through the last time."

"Thank you, ma'am," Amanda replied. "He speaks highly of both you and your husband."

"Have you had any trouble with Indian raids lately?" Jim asked, with a serious look on his face.

"Not really," Mrs. Bauer answered. "A horse is stolen every once in a while, and that's about it. They don't bother the cattle unless they are trying to get revenge for something where they feel they've been wronged."

"That's good," Jim replied. "I'm glad to hear that. Amanda and I are headed to Runnels county to start a ranch. We've got twenty-seven head of cattle, a team of horses, and eight Rangers to help us get them there. I just came by to introduce you to Amanda and make sure you're alright. Tell your husband we said hello and please come by and say hello if you're ever close to Ballinger."

Mrs. Bauer promised they would and thanked Jim for stopping by to check on them. She was happy that so many good things had happened for him since they met the first time. After all Jim had done for her and her husband, she thought he deserved the world.

36

JIM MEETS LONE EAGLE

Jim and Amanda climbed back on the wagon and started a slow trot to catch up with the Rangers and cattle. Again, the drive proved uneventful until just before they got to Runnels county. It was then that about twenty-five Indians showed up and rode on the southern side of the herd. The outriders had seen them and warned Jim and the rest of the party. Jim brought the herd in close to the wagon and everyone was issued a Winchester repeating rifle and lots of ammunition.

One Indian with a headdress, presumably the chief, rode in and asked one of the Rangers for a parley. Jim asked the Ranger what he thought and the Ranger replied that he thought it was a good idea to parley. It couldn't hurt to talk, the Ranger reasoned. If things didn't go well, they were prepared to fight.

The chief introduced himself as Lone Eagle. He was a Comanche who had been with Quanah Parker and his band, but had not been present at the Palo Duro fight.

"We slipped away the night before the battle and were trying to make it to Mexico," the chief told Jim and the Ranger. "We are hungry, the buffalo are gone, and we have not been able to provide enough by hunting alone. We have some guns, but little ammunition. If you could help us, we would be forever grateful."

Jim could see the sincerity in the chief's eyes and sense the hunger in his voice.

"What do you need?" Jim asked the chief.

"I have fifty braves who have not eaten for three or four days," Lone Eagle replied. "We need some of your beeves for food."

"How many do you think would sustain you?" Jim asked.

"We need ten head of cattle to keep going," the chief replied.

"I can give you five. If I gave you more, I wouldn't have enough to start my ranch in Runnels county," Jim told him.

"Alright," Lone Wolf sadly replied. "We will do everything we can to make five cattle do."

The Rangers cut out five heifers and the Indians drove them off as they left the area.

"This will cut down our herd, but it probably saved our lives," Jim told Amanda before adding, "I'll bet we haven't heard the last from Chief Lone Wolf."

"His name was Lone Eagle," Amanda said, laughing.

"I'm a little nervous," Jim replied, smiling. "Alright...I bet this isn't the last we've heard from Lone *Eagle*."

Jim was right. In the coming years, when the chief made his trips from the Llano Estacada in far west Texas on his way to Mexico, he would stop by the ranch and spend a day or two. The Walkers would always have a big celebration with a barbecue to welcome their friend. On each visit, Jim would allow Lone Eagle and his braves to take five head of cattle as a remembrance of the first time they met on the Walkers' first trek to their ranch in Runnels county.

After meeting Lone Eagle and giving him the cattle, Jim asked Amanda if he could drive the wagon on to Ballinger while he went ahead to make arrangements for their arrival. He needed to buy some fence posts since the cattle needed to be penned in a corral until a larger pasture was fenced. Jim also wanted to check on the progression of the Indian problem that was supposed to have been solved since they last time he had visited.

Amanda agreed to his request.

"I'll only be an hour or so behind you," she told Jim with a grin. "I'll be alright. I have eight young Texas Rangers to keep me company while you're gone!"

"Alright, alright," Jim said, laughing. "I'll hurry!"

When Jim got to Ballinger, he went directly to the Paskel Land Company, where he found Kim, sitting tall behind the counter. Jim asked for Mr. Paskel but was told he would not be back until early afternoon.

"Can I help?" She asked.

"Well, the JVA Cattle Company is about to arrive with twenty heifers, two bulls, four draft horses, a wagon loaded with equipment, and eight Texas Rangers acting as drovers. I need to buy some fence posts and wire."

"There's a new invention called barbed wire you ought to look into," Kim told him. "You can buy that at the hardware store and your fence posts at the lumber company here in town."

"I also lost part of my herd by using them as a bargaining tool with some Indians we met on our way," Jim said. "I believe that trade saved our lives. Your boss has assured me the Indian threat here in Ballinger is pretty much over."

With that, they both looked out the window to see cattle kicking up dust as the wagon and livestock entered the town square.

"Kim," Jim said with a smile on his face, "you are now looking at the whole of JWA Cattle Company...and the beautiful lady driving the wagon is my new wife, Amanda."

With that, Jim ran out to the wagon and told Amanda that he had to go by the lumber company to check on fence posts and the hardware store to check on wire.

"Climb on board and tell me where to go," Amanda replied.

"I'm not completely sure," Jim said, looking around, "but I think the lumber company is on the second block off the square and the hardware store is about two blocks north of the lumber company. Let's go and see if we can find them."

Before leaving, Jim told the Rangers to hold the cattle on the square until they could drive them to the ranch. At the lumber company and hardware store, he purchased enough posts for the corral and enough wire for both the corral and big pasture. As it was getting toward night, they decided to camp their cattle and hobble their horses.

They went back to the town square and picked up the Rangers and their cattle. He hoped he could find the future home of JWA Cattle Company. He remembered it was more or less five miles north of town with a large creek and a clump of giant oak and cottonwood trees where he thought the main house and headquarters would be, subject to Amanda's approval.

37

THEIR NEW HOME

Mr. Paskel had placed markers on each corner of the land to denote property boundaries. When Jim and Amanda came over the rise, the sun just going down behind the giant oak trees. The view before them looked like a masterpiece painted by an artist.

"Well, this is where I thought the headquarters for JWA should be – right there among those oak trees. What do you think? Do you like it?" Jim said, reaching over and squeezing Amanda's hand excitedly.

"Oh, Jim!" she exclaimed. "It's absolutely beautiful!"

"You're right," Jim told her, still holding her hand, "but not near as beautiful as you. Nothing is as beautiful as you."

Jim looked into her eyes and pulled her close.

"Thank you for being here and sharing this moment with me," he told her. "I will treasure it forever."

Amanda beamed.

"I never thought I could have feelings for another woman after Laurie," Jim said, after pausing a bit. "She was my life and the mother of my children. Don't be jealous of my feelings for her, though, as she would not be jealous of you. She would want me to move on and find someone as wonderful as you...and there's one thing I know for sure: that I'm the luckiest person in the whole wide world and I love you with all my heart!"

After sharing a moment together and taking everything in, he smiled.

"There's just one thing I've been pondering this whole trip," Jim said with mock contemplation. "Should we change the name of JW Cattle Company to JAW or even AJW Cattle Company?"

"No!" She laughed. "Just leave it as it is! You started it and got it going! I want to see if this place is successful before I put my initials into it!"

They both laughed and then went to work unloading the wagon.

Jim and Amanda had not had much privacy during their marriage and it didn't look as if that would change any time in the near future. The headquarters for the JWA Cattle Company was currently a bare prairie with oak and cottonwood trees and a running creek. That was fine for old married folks, but not for two newlyweds. To make things worse, there were not any hotels or any other places where they could find privacy nearby.

The next three weeks were spent in a frenzy. The Rangers spent the time building a log cabin with a cellar underneath with a staircase and a trap door. The house was long with two bedrooms on one end and a kitchen and family room on the other. Each end had a pot-bellied stove to provide heat. They had even found good water when they struck an artesian aquifer at about twenty feet below the surface of their land.

The corral was built with a lean-to shelter to protect the livestock with enough storage for the livestock feed. The last week of setting up the ranch was spent with all hands on deck including Jim and sometimes Amanda building the fence around the perimeter of the two hundred acres with a cross fence to protect the cultivated region.

At the end of three busy but productive weeks, Jim and Amanda cooked a really big meal and held a thank-you celebration for the Rangers. Jim gave each of them ten dollars, which totaled a regular month's pay for them. He also wrote a sincere letter of gratitude to Mr. and Mrs. Spillar and promised to repay them for their kindness. He also told the Rangers they always had a place to stay any time they were scouting nearby.

When the Rangers rode off back to Mexia, Jim and Amanda felt lost in happiness as everything had gone better than they could have expected.

They were also going to be alone for the first time since they married on what seemed like a Friday night so long ago. It was a happy time.

At the end of the first year, there was a full crop of calves and a new member of the Walker family. Little Ruth had come to live with her dad and new stepmother for the first time since Jim had set out to retrieve Bobby's body. On a trip back to Mexia, Jim and Amanda visited the Pruitts so they could bring Little Ruth home with them. Though the Pruitts knew this day would come, it was a sad occasion for them and Little Ruth, too. Ruth had come to look upon them as a mother and father and wasn't used to seeing Jim hardly at all. Amanda was pregnant with their first child at the time and Jim joked he hoped it would be a boy to help him out around the newly formed JWA Cattle Company.

When the baby arrived, it was a girl. As soon as Jim looked into her big blue eyes, he couldn't help but fall in love with her.

"I guess I can handle the workload a little longer," he said grinning and holding the sweet new arrival in his arms.

Amanda said she wanted to name the little girl Addie Bernice and Jim agreed on what he thought was a beautiful name.

Soon after the birth, Amanda leaned into Jim after the children had fallen asleep one night.

"Jim, I've got a secret I think you should know," she said quietly.

"I think this is as good a time as any to get all these secrets out in the open," Jim said, chuckling.

Amanda bowed her hand slightly.

"Well, out with it!" He said nudging her.

"My name isn't really Amanda," she said sheepishly. "Or at least it's not quite just that."

"Wow, that's a deep dark secret," Jim said, pulling her close. "Tell me everything, girl!"

"My full name is Barbara Amanda Victoria Hughes Walker," she replied looking up at him.

"Wow," Jim said smiling. "That is a beautiful name for a gorgeous woman."

The following year was a frenzy of activity with a lot accomplished, but never enough. There was so much to do and never enough time. But, the Walkers had fun. They were well on their way to repaying the Spillars and had acquired two more acres of land and transferred it from raw prairie into well-manicured farmland. If not for the lingering nuisance of raiding Indians, everything would have been absolutely perfect.

38

A KILLING RAID

One morning Amanda was on the back porch and saw several riders sauntering across the prairie. She guessed they were roughly a mile away and heading toward their ranch, but didn't seem to be in a big hurry.

Little Ruth and two neighbor girls were playing in the backyard while the new baby, Addie Bernice, was sleeping in the bedroom. Jim was talking with the father of the neighbor girls, a man named Philip Hobson. While checking the Walkers' cattle, they noticed that someone had cut the fences the night before, allowing their cattle to get out of their pastures.

After following the cattle and some unshod pony tracks for a long and exhausting distance, the missing cattle were found. Unfortunately, several of the cows were dead with spears in their bodies.

"Why would they do that?" Philip asked. "Cattle are no good to them dead."

"Because they don't like cattle," Jim replied. "It's merely a ploy to draw us away from our places while our women and children are unprotected there."

"Oh, Lord!" Philip exclaimed. "My poor wife and children!"

"These are Indians on a killing raid," Jim said seriously, with fear in his eyes. "I'm afraid you're right! You go to your house and I'll go to mine. If you family is alright, you come to my house and I'll do the same!"

Back near the house, Amanda screamed to Philip's wife, Nancy.

"Grab the girls and get into the underground room!" She yelled frantically. "I've already put Addie in her basket down there. Thankfully, she is asleep! Instruct those girls to be as quiet as a mouse! These are bad, bad people!"

Before going into the underground room, Amanda grabbed four Winchester Repeating Rifles and four boxes of ammunition. She almost fell going down the stairs to the cellar beneath the ranch house. Luckily, Mrs. Hobson was a crack shot, as was Little Ruth. Amanda assumed the Hobson girl was, too, when she grabbed the fourth rifle. In those parts of Texas, it was necessary for both women and children to be well-trained in firearms and horsemanship.

Amanda handed the rifles to each of the girls and Mrs. Hobson. She had left the front door open and the window shades up so she could see what the Indians were doing outside the house. Running back up the stairs, she grabbed another repeater and four more boxes of shells. She was preparing for a long siege and was quite concerned for Jim and Philip.

When she looked out the window, she noticed they had stopped at the barn and were looking in her direction. She hurriedly left the trap door about halfway up and stood on the stairs so she could see their movement. About ten of the Indians from the larger group rode up to the house and stopped at the edge of the open porch. She could see them, but they couldn't see her. She was scared that the baby would wake up and start crying, alerting the Indians to their presence in the house. After what seemed like a lifetime, but was probably no more than ten minutes, they rode off and joined the larger group at the barn.

Amanda guessed they were trying to decide their strategy. She knew they were going to attack. It was just a matter of when and how. Just then several rifle shots were heard and Amanda pushed up the door and saw Jim riding hard toward the house. He had surprised the Indians who had not had time to react and stop him from reaching the house. When he reached the home, he jumped off his mount and raced for the front door Amanda had left open.

With Jim there, the strategy of protection changed completely. The Walkers had six rifles and a stockpile of ammunition. One of these rifles, however, had been left in the saddle scabbard when Jim jumped off his horse onto the porch. Still, what they had should have been enough firepower. They decided that someone should watch all sides of the house and direct their fire in the direction most needed.

After about half an hour, a lone rider was seen riding like the wind toward the house. It was Philip coming up from the Hobson place to join in the fight. He didn't know where his family was at that time, but was thrilled to find them safe with the Walkers.

Jim greeted Philip and was happy to see him safe and sound.

"I think our best strategy would be to shoot their horses. They are easier to hit and that will thwart an attack," Jim told Philip as soon as he arrived. "Comanche Indians are the best light cavalry in the world when mounted, but are not as effective on foot. So, aim for the horse. We've got to keep them at a distance so they don't get close enough to set the house on fire."

"I can hit what looks like the chief with that feathered headdress," Philip said, looking out toward the raiding Indians.

"No," Jim stopped him. "Let's make them start the ruckus. Maybe they'll just go away. It's not likely, but there's always a chance."

Jim asked Amanda to fetch their field glasses. Once he had them, Jim surveyed the scene outside for about ten minutes.

"There seems to be an argument of some sort between the chief and younger braves," Jim told them, "and it looks like the chief is losing."

"Can they win this fight?" Philip asked, saying aloud what everyone else had been wondering.

Jim, who had been in many skirmishes, spoke with a bit of resignation in his voice.

"They certainly have the numbers on their side," he replied grimly, "but the cost of their victory would be high. I imagine that's what the chief and braves have been arguing about. The old chief probably wants to go find easier pickings."

They chuckled in an attempt to mask their fear, but they were in a world of hurt and needed help. They just didn't know where the help would come from.

At about four o'clock, Jim and Philip decided that if the Indians didn't attack in the next hour, they would fire on the group at the barn if they were still there. They wanted it all over by dark, one way or the other.

At about four-thirty, the Indians began to line up their ponies facing the front of the ranch house. Seeing this, Jim alerted everyone to get into position, check their weapons, and be ready. One of the younger braves was directing the attack when they came riding hard toward the ranch house.

"Hold your fire until I give you the order to shoot and remember to shoot the horses," Jim told them all. "Have your targets picked out before you fire and when you run out of shells, the girls should have another rifle loaded and ready for you."

When the first wave was roughly fifty feet away, Jim gave the order to fire. The Indians melted away like wheat cut by a sickle under the scalding fire. Another wave was ordered forward with the same results. Not many Indians were killed as they neared the ranch house, but they were without their horses.

The attacks stopped for a time while the young braves seemed to clamber for another frontal attack. Jim estimated that they had time for one more assault before darkness set in. He had heard that, for the most part, Indians did not like to fight at night. He wasn't sure if there was any truth to that, though, or if it was just an old wive's tale. He was hoping it was true.

As nighttime fell, the Indians built large campfires near the barn and the corral. With the brightness of the large fires, you could see their activities from the house, but they didn't create any hostility toward the ranch house during that time.

The night was spent trying to devise a better strategy for the defense come daylight. The Indians evidently were not going anywhere and it seemed they were willing to pay the price for victory, no matter what it might be. Sleeping in shifts, rest did not come easy for those in the house that night.

39

THE ARRIVAL OF LONE EAGLE

When the first rays of daylight came streaking across the night sky, everyone knew it was time to prepare themselves for the possibility of another fight. As the sun started rising over the trees in the east, they saw a hazy line of what appeared to be horses and riders stretching as far as the eye could see. The Indians had received reinforcements during the night and now it seemed even more hopeless than before.

When Jim looked out, he noticed that the new batch of Indians were probably more than a mile away and didn't appear to be joining up with the others at the barn.

Philip and Jim discussed how to best defend the homestead when a small party of new arrivals came riding straight for the house. The men didn't really know what to make of the situation, but they were scared. A chief appeared to be leading the group.

When the Indians didn't veer off to meet the others at the barn and kept coming straight for the house, Jim wasn't concerned anymore. He was confused. When the

Indians got within fifty yards in the dim light, he thought he recognized his old friend, Lone Eagle. As the group drew closer, he was sure it was him.

With his arm raised over his head indicating a sign of peace, Lone Eagle rode up to the porch and dismounted. He walked through the door and made the universal peace sign so that everyone could see.

"Good friend, Jim Walker," the chief said, approaching the men. "We've come to help. A group of renegade Apache, Kiowa, and Comanches have left the reservation at Fort Sill on a murder raid. A chief's son was killed by a drunken white man over in Big Springs and he is seeking revenge. You can see he is the one at the barn with the headdress on."

Jim and Philip looked toward the barn and saw the chief there, again talking with the braves.

"I'm going to go down and try to reason with him," Lone Eagle told them. "If reasoning does not work, we will fight him. Jim Walker is my friend."

"We are so grateful," Jim replied thankfully. "We will go with you to talk to the chief."

"No," Lone Eagle replied. "He is an old friend who has let his grief control him. For his sake and the sake of the tribe, he must go back to the reservation and take his young braves with him. Stay inside the house and close all your windows and doors until this is over. It should not take long for this to be settled."

The chief briskly walked out the door and mounted his horse. Jim and Philip watched as he rode slowly down to the barn and raised his hand in greeting to his old friend. After saying hello, they moved away from the main group and talked, just the two of them. Every once in a while, a young brave would wander over and make some animated arm gestures, but appeared to be rebuked by the old chief.

After a period of time, the two chiefs stood facing each other and each placed a hand on the shoulder of the other. It seemed they had come to an agreement that was acceptable to them both. The old chief then went over to his group of braves at the barn while Lone Eagle mounted his horse and started riding back to the ranch house.

After tying his horse to the railing, Lone Eagle came to the door where he met Philip and Jim.

"I have promised the chief that you will give him twenty head of cattle to feed his braves," Lone Eagle told Jim. "That is a much better deal than losing our scalps *and* all of our cattle, isn't it?"

"I will furnish half those cattle," Philip spoke up.

"And we will also give some beeves to you and your braves, old friend," Jim said gratefully. "You have most assuredly saved our lives."

Lone Eagle nodded his thanks.

"If you are willing to stay around, I am sure I could get some of the other ranchers in the area to contribute some cattle," Jim added. "You know, you and your braves could drive the livestock up across the Red River and start your own ranch. I've heard that's what Quanah Parker did and he's been quite successful."

The next week was spent riding from ranch to ranch explaining the plan to supply Lone Eagle and his band with seed cattle to start ranching activities in the Indian territory. Jim knew Burk Burnett and Waggoner and other big ranchers had advised Quanah Parker in running a successful ranch. As the ranchers had said, it was simply an investment to protect their own herds. The Indians were going from cattle rustlers to cattle raisers.

As the Walker and Hobson families watched Lone Eagle ride off with his braves, they knew that a way of life with which they had lived so long was coming to an end.

Since the Indians' discovery of the horse that was brought to Texas by Spanish conquistadors, they had become almost impossible to defeat. Then, when the white man entered the area in the early 1820's, the Indians remained unconquerable until the Battle of Palo Duro Canyon in the 1870's. The Indians were only beaten then because they had been separated from their horse herd.

For half a century, the Indians had reigned supreme. It was the longest war the country had ever fought and men like Jim Walker had played a big role in it over and over again. _____

EPILOGUE

JIM REFLECTS ON HIS LIFE

The next few years went by quickly and the Walker family moved into a new and larger rock and plank house with water inside supplied by a windmill. Jim had repaid Mr. Spillar monetarily, but he could never repay him for all he had done. Since starting his ranch, he had acquired over twenty-five thousand acres of land through purchase or binding option to purchase. He also had roughly five thousand head of San Gertrudis cattle, a new breed that had been developed on the King Ranch. Life was good and Jim knew he and his family had been lucky. Of course, everything they had was the result of hard work, a labor of love, by both him and Amanda. But, as Amanda reminded him, also a little bit of luck. Of course, she always said, the harder you worked, the luckier you got.

Amanda and Jim had five additional children with three boys and two little girls. Little Ruth rounded the out the family as the sixth and oldest child. And, to Amanda's undying credit, she never let Little Ruth forget who her real mother was or how wonderful she was and how much she had loved her.

Amanda home-schooled all the children and Little Ruth went on to pass her college entrance exam at Baylor University and eventually her entrance exam to obtain her law degree from Baylor in Waco. Following that, she opened a law office in Waco and served two terms as a state representative from her local district. She handled all the legal matters of the ranch, which filled most of her time. She remained a single woman for a long time, saying she wouldn't marry until she had enough time to devote to a man, but she felt she would eventually.

Three of her brothers and sisters had spent four wonderful years at Texas A&M and one was a junior enrolled at the University of Texas at Austin. Jim and Amanda were very proud of their children and rightfully so.

The Walker family had suffered the hardships and privations of early childhood and had become hard-working, responsible young adults. They were a credit to themselves and their community.

The older children experienced the hardships that a new country necessitates. This put more stiffness in their backbone and enabled them to meet life's challenges.

Jim had been approached many times about running for Congress and Governor of the state, but he felt could be more beneficial helping guide organizations such as the Southwestern Cattleman's Association, the Quarter Horse Association, and other grass roots groups in the area. He also loved to cross breed cattle and was always aiming to create a better, fatter, and hardier breed of livestock.

Jim never felt special. He had been fortunate to have such special friends as the Spillars, the Pruitts, and two of the most beautiful and gracious wives in the world. The one regret he had in his life was losing Bobby in Tennessee. He had never gotten over that loss and was forever sorry that he didn't bring Bobby's body back while his mother and dad were still alive. He continually carried the burden of convincing a reluctant Bobby into going back into the 10th Texas before the last battle of Franklin. Every fifth year on the anniversary of the battle, Jim went to visit West Columbia to visit Bobby's grave. It always made him feel melancholy, but he felt he owed it to his friend. He would sometimes wonder why a good person like Bobby had died so early while he had enjoyed such a full and wonderful life. It didn't seem fair.

Jim and Amanda also reflected often on their inability to share their children with their grandparents in Mississippi. Due to the war and distance, it hadn't been possible to keep from shutting them out of their lives. This bothered them both, especially Jim, quite a bit.

Overall, Jim loved his life and much of that was because he got to live as a rancher. He loved to sit on the front porch of their house and remember the days of his youth, his coming to Texas, and the unbelievable adventures he had experienced as an adult. He was grateful for everything he had been through and every gift he had been given.

All the time, God was good.

God was good all the time.

Printed in the United States
By Bookmasters